D0398222

KNOCKOUT
ENTREPRENEUR

KNOCKOUT
ENTREPRENEUR

GEORGE FOREMAN
WITH KEN ABRAHAM

THOMAS NELSON
Since 1798

NASHVILLE   DALLAS   MEXICO CITY   RIO DE JANEIRO   BEIJING

Published in Nashville, Tennessee, by Thomas Nelson. Thomas Nelson is a registered trademark of Thomas Nelson, Inc.

Published in association with the literary agency of Mark Sweeney & Associates, Bonita Springs, Florida 34135.

Thomas Nelson, Inc., titles may be purchased in bulk for educational, business, fund-raising, or sales promotional use. For information, please e-mail SpecialMarkets@ThomasNelson.com.

Unless otherwise noted, Scripture quotations are taken from THE NEW KING JAMES VERSION. © 1982 by Thomas Nelson, Inc. Used by permission. All rights reserved.

Scripture quotations noted NASB are taken from the NEW AMERICAN STANDARD BIBLE®, © The Lockman Foundation 1960, 1962, 1963, 1968, 1971, 1972, 1973, 1975, 1977, 1995. Used by permission.

Scripture quotations noted KJV are taken from the KING JAMES VERSION.

Library of Congress Cataloging-in-Publication Data

Foreman, George, 1949–
   The knockout entrepreneur : a champion's secrets to success, happiness, and significance / George Foreman with Ken Abraham.
      p. cm.
   Includes bibliographical references.
   ISBN 978-0-7852-2208-8 (hardcover)
   1. Entrepreneurship. 2. Success in business. 3. Success. I. Abraham, Ken. II. Title.
   HB615.F675 2009
   658.4'09—dc22

                              2009014648

Printed in the United States of America

09 10 11 12 13 QW 7 6 5 4 3 2

CONTENTS

This book is about success and significance—not just mine, but yours! Whether you are starting a business, trying to revitalize your career, or taking an existing business to the next level of success, the principles I'm going to share with you in the following pages work. I can assure you of that because these are the principles by which I have run my business and my life. They are also some of the most important truths I have taught—and continue to teach—my ten children. And you *know* I want them to succeed and make their mark in this world.

What is a Knockout Entrepreneur? He or she is a person who truly wants to succeed in life and is willing to do the hard work necessary to make it happen.

He sees an opportunity to grow or prosper and seizes it. He is a person who believes that a new thing not only needs to be done but *can* be done. He dreams of managing his own life and career well, but he doesn't stop there. He or she is a pioneer, an adventurer, a trailblazer; she is a person with a new idea; he is a visionary who can see beyond the barriers created by unmerited loyalty to the same old "stuck in the mud" concepts. He or she is a person who wants to explore the possibilities, to improve the status quo.

A Knockout Entrepreneur may or may not be an inventor; in fact, most are not. I'm not an inventor, but I've learned to recognize a good idea when I see one. Instead, the Knockout Entrepreneur may be a carpenter or an accountant, a building contractor, a computer technician, a songwriter, or a hair stylist. But all are men and women of integrity who do quality work. Their reputations precede them and draw more chances to succeed their way.

Many Knockout Entrepreneurs take something that already exists and they find ways to make it better, more pleasing or useful to a wider segment of the public, or they make it function easier. Oftentimes in doing so, they find new career opportunities for themselves. The best Knockout Entrepreneurs have found a way to serve others and as a result discover their greatest fulfillment.

The most common characteristic of a Knockout Entrepreneur is that he or she is a risk-taker; he or she is willing to assume the calculated risk of stepping into new territory, exploring potential and possibilities, knowing full well that not everything is going to work out wonderfully, but something will. He wants to move up in the world; she wants to be her own boss, to run her own business, or at least be in charge of her section of the world.

And a Knockout Entrepreneur is the person who gets the job done. He or she is not content to say, "Well, I tried, and it didn't work." He will keep fighting until he knocks out the obstacles barring him from success, whether it is fear, lack of education, insufficient skills, doubt, that "you'll never amount to anything" attitude, financial or family stress, or entrenched community attitudes. Whatever the opposition, the Knockout Entrepreneur is the person who stays in the ring and will not give up, no matter how many times he or she gets knocked down. He will get back up and give that idea another shot, or take a new route, perhaps looking at it from a new perspective; she will examine her mistakes and find ways to improve. If everything else fails, the Knockout Entrepreneur will apply the lessons learned, say good-bye to the past, and move on with hope in his heart and a positive attitude. Knockout Entrepreneurs are winners, but not because everything they touch turns to gold. They are successful because they overcome the challenges they face in their individual "rings."

ALL THE MONEY YOU NEED—AND MORE!

Throughout this book I'll share with you what my kids call "Georgisms," the ideas and principles I constantly try to impart to them, truths they can use in their everyday lives to help guide them to success. As I share these ideas, please understand that I'm talking about much more than money. Certainly I want you to have all the money you need, but I want to help you discover more success in every area of your life.

Funny thing about success: for many people, attaining it is as difficult and elusive as trying to capture fog in a bottle. They think that success is possible only for the elite few. But success is not reserved for talented athletes, extra-ordinarily gifted artists, or brilliant businesspeople. It is available to those people who are willing to use their God-given imaginations and work hard over the long haul to achieve their goals. Most men and women, I'm convinced, are not working anywhere near their potential; they have settled for far less than what they can do, what they can have, and most important, who they can be.

But don't be fooled. While success is available to anyone, it does not happen easily; nor does it happen overnight. Most overnight successes—people who suddenly burst onto the scene and seem to have King Midas's golden touch—have been working toward their goals for years.

Understand, success in your business or career does not automatically translate to success in other aspects of your life. In fact, if you don't handle your business success well, it can work against your relationships, your health, and your mental attitudes. It is almost universally true that someone who is unhappy with his career will not be much fun to live with at home. Truth is, failure at your work almost always contributes to unhappiness in your heart and mind and inevitably spills over onto the people closest to you. On the other hand, if you find satisfaction and a sense of fulfillment in your career, even if it does not make you fabulously wealthy from a financial standpoint, your life will be rich in many other ways and you will be much more likely to enjoy your family, your friends, and other aspects of life. That's one reason why my goal is your success. I know that if you are more successful, you are going to be happier and the people around you are going to see and feel the effects.

Sometimes it helps, though, to receive encouragement or advice from someone else doing something similar to what you are doing. In the pages ahead I'll let you in on my personal secrets of success, and I'll give you specific strategies for competing and winning against any competition. As you incorporate these ideas into your plans, you too can be a Knockout Entrepreneur!

CHAPTER ONE

SEE WHAT CAN BE

C an you imagine turning down more than $100 million? I almost did. Not directly, of course. Nobody came up and offered me that kind of cash on the spot. But I nearly missed one of the greatest entrepreneurial opportunities of the twentieth century when I told my friend I wasn't interested in his portable electric grill. You've probably seen George Foreman's Lean, Mean, Fat-Reducing Grilling Machine, a handsomely packaged product (with my picture on the box, of course), with sleek, efficient qualities that make grilling on your kitchen counter a snap and cleanup even easier. Best of all, the food tastes fantastic because the grill seals in the food's natural juices as it cooks.

But when I first saw the grill, it didn't look at all like it does today. It looked more like a clunky steel box. I couldn't imagine anyone wanting one of those things in his home. Consequently, I could not see the grill's *potential*. Success doesn't always come to you wrapped in a pretty package. More often you have to look past what *is* to recognize what an opportunity *can be*. But I hadn't learned that yet.

I had already won a gold medal for boxing in the 1968 Olympics held in Mexico City; then I turned professional and won the title of heavyweight champion of the world just a few years later. Now I was working on a comeback career, hoping to do what no boxer had ever done before—to win the heavyweight championship in my forties!

Because of my boxing success, I had appeared in a couple of television commercials, and I had promoted a few products of my own on the market, but nothing that had become a household name. Nevertheless, I was always glad when somebody wanted to pay me to attach my name to an excellent product. For instance, I was relaxing at home one day when the telephone rang. The caller said, "We're trying to find George Foreman."

Since I wasn't sure of his intentions, I asked, "May I ask why you need to talk to George Foreman?"

"We're trying to put a commercial together and want to talk to him about it."

"Oh! This is George!"

"Are you really George Foreman, the boxer?" the caller asked.

"Yes, this is George Foreman, the boxer."

"Great, I'm glad I found you! Nike is making a shoe commercial and wants you to be in it."

"A shoe commercial? Really?" I had never been in a Nike commercial before.

"It's not much money," he continued, "but it won't take a lot of your time either."

A few years earlier I was flat broke and barely making any money at all before my boxing comeback. When this fellow mentioned the low compensation they were offering, I thought, *You don't know what "not much money" means. There was a time when five dollars sounded like a lot of money to me!* Of course, I didn't say that to the man on the phone.

Instead I said, "Sure, I'll be glad to work with you."

I did the commercial with pro football running back Bo Jackson, who was already a household name because of his "Bo knows" commercials. Nike was looking for a fresh way to use Bo Jackson, so in the spot a group of reporters asked Bo several questions about running. Since Bo knows everything about anything, they expected him to answer all their questions. Pretending to be irritated, he said, "Look, I don't have time for all this stuff!"

Just then I jumped out of nowhere and shouted, "But I do!" And then I started dancing across the floor. The point was that the young athlete was too tired to play, but George Foreman, the forty-year-old "retired" athlete, was full of energy and still wanted to make things happen (with the help of Nike products). We had a lot of fun shooting the commercial, and the public really connected with it. People loved it, and they started calling out my name everywhere I went: "Hey, George! I saw you on the commercial with Bo."

The Nike commercial led to a McDonald's commercial. Everyone knew I liked to eat cheeseburgers, so when I was making my return to boxing, the reporters often teased me about eating so much. Some people even called me "the cheeseburger guy."

"George isn't the prodigal son of boxing," one wag said. "He's the fatted calf!" Another commented, "George Foreman has his training camp right next to Burger King." Someone else said, "George can't be the heavyweight champ of the world again as long as his training camp is at Baskin-Robbins."

I teased right back with the press. When someone asked me why I was still boxing in my forties, I said, "I've got to keep fighting because it's the only thing that keeps me out of the hamburger joints!"

A reporter asked me to sample all the hamburgers in various fast-food restaurants, ranking the burgers on a scale from one to ten, with ten being the best-tasting hamburger. When I graded the burgers, I didn't rank McDonald's as high as some of the others. In fact, I placed Wendy's burgers high above those of the Golden Arches.

Somebody at McDonald's got word of my "scientific research." Not to be outdone, McDonald's called me for an endorsement and created a special George Foreman burger, which I promoted on television. In return, McDonald's donated an electronic scoreboard for the youth center I had opened in the inner-city section of Houston.

Then I did a commercial for Doritos. After that I endorsed Oscar Mayer wieners. Then Kentucky Fried Chicken. I didn't want to be known only for food commercials—although I enjoyed them quite a bit—so I branched out to other products as the opportunities came along. In a Motel 6 commercial, I popped out of a suitcase. I've also done ads for Meineke Car Care. I was the guy who growled loudly, "I am not going to pay a lot for this muffler!" Surprised at the quality and price of the Meineke muffler, I always went away happy. I have also done commercials for Casual Male Big & Tall clothes and others.

HOW THE GEORGE FOREMAN LEAN, MEAN, FAT-REDUCING GRILLING MACHINE CAME TO BE

Then one day an attorney friend came to me with an offer. He said, "George, there are some guys who want to talk with you. You've helped other companies by advertising their products. Have you ever thought about having your own product?"

"Okay," I replied. "How much are they willing to pay me?" I had been making a lot of money doing endorsements for various products, so that's what first came to mind.

"No, no. They're not going to pay you anything," the attorney answered. "There's no money up front. It will be a joint venture. You'll get your own product, and we can help you promote it."

"What? No money up front?"

I thought, *With all the money I'm making with endorsements, I'm not going to do anything without getting paid. I'd be undermining the value of my own endorsement.*

"Just look at it," the attorney urged. Later he sent me a small slanted grill and asked me to try it out.

I looked at it and said, "Mmm, that's nice." I put it back in the box, got busy with other things, and forgot all about it.

A couple of months later my friend called back. "George, how do you like the grill?"

"Oh, the grill. To be honest, I haven't tried it yet. Let me get back with you on that."

"George, they need to know something."

Right then I almost made one of the worst financial decisions I could have made. I thought, *I really don't have time for this.*

Fortunately my wife, Joan, was listening and she changed my mind. "I've tried the grill, George," Joan said, "and I like it a lot. It works great; the meat comes out nice and juicy. The grease drips right off, and the food tastes really good."

"Are you serious?"

"Yeah," she replied. "I'll fix you a burger."

After taking a bite I realized Joan was right. I said, "Yeah, it is really good. And the grill is easy to clean up. I like this grill!"

When I talked to the attorney again, I said, "I'll do it!" I wasn't thinking about making any money on the deal. I just signed the contract so I could get sixteen free grills for my homes, my training camp, my friends, my mom, cousins, and other family members. That's all I really expected to get out of the grill deal. I never dreamed this opportunity would turn into a grilling empire!

After I made the first commercials and infomercial to advertise the grill, sales skyrocketed. People would see me in an airport and call out, "Hey, George, we love you, man!"

"Oh, did you see me fight?" I'd ask.

"No, we bought one of your grills."

Somebody else said, "My doctor told me to get your grill because it might help me lower my cholesterol."

"Did it help?" I asked.

"I don't know, but I'm sure eatin' better!"

Another person said that the grill helped him with diabetes and heart problems because the fat drained off the meat so well.

We were ecstatic when we sold 1 million grills. Then sales hit 5 million. Soon 10 million grills sold. It became so popular that Salton, the appliance maker, offered to pay me a fortune for my rights to the George Foreman grill.

Today, more than 100 million George Foreman grills have been sold worldwide. It won't be long before sales surge past the 150 million mark. And it all started when a friend asked me to consider an interesting opportunity.

I give my wife, Joan, credit for the success of the George Foreman grill because she was the first one to use the product and she sold *me* on it. She saw the grill's potential before I did, and I'm glad I listened to her. That one decision not only blessed my life but also improved the lives of millions of other people. My family has prospered, and as a result we've been able to help a lot of other families prosper. Not only that, but a lot of people who have purchased George Foreman grills are enjoying some fine eating! You never know how making one small decision can change so many lives.

Just because an opportunity doesn't pique my imagination or look too exciting at first, I've learned not to discount it. Sometimes all sorts of blessings are right behind an unopened door, but you'll never know until you open it. If you want to be successful, you must think in terms of potential. Don't limit yourself to what the opportunity is, but allow yourself to dream a bit about what the opportunity can be.

WHEN ONE DREAM ENDS, DREAM ANOTHER

When I realized what a great product the grill was, I promoted it passionately. I could tell that my boxing career was winding down, but my career as a pitchman for the grill was on its way up, so I talked about the grill everywhere I went—even at boxing matches! For instance, I fought my last boxing match against Shannon Briggs at Trump Taj Mahal in Atlantic City in November 1997. Shannon was twenty-five years of age with orange dreadlocks, and I was forty-eight and bald. He weighed 227 pounds, and I weighed 260. Shannon Briggs had won thirty fights, with one loss and twenty-four knockouts; I had won seventy-six matches, with four losses and sixty-eight knockouts. Plus, by then I had won boxing's most prestigious title—heavyweight champion of the world—twice, the second time at forty-five years of age.

When the fight began, Briggs came out quickly, snapping a sharp left jab. He caught me with that jab at least twice in the first round, and it really hurt. But when the bell rang, I went back to my corner and stood—just as I had for every fight since my return to boxing ten years earlier—while my opponent sat down and rested. My trainer, Angelo Dundee, gave me some water and I was ready to go back to work.

The bell rang for round two. Briggs came out fast again, but halfway through the round, I connected with three left jabs as I continued pressing toward Briggs, who was backpedaling. The younger, faster fighter kept trying to move away from me, but I advanced on him anytime I could. The match continued like that for the first five rounds with me constantly applying the pressure. Toward the end of the sixth, though, Briggs bounced several blows off my shaved head and a couple into my face, causing my eyes to swell a bit.

By the eighth round, Briggs must have thought I was getting tired—I wasn't. I connected with numerous hard punches, one of which was a straight shot to Shannon's jaw. *Craackk!* All over the arena the crowd heard the blow and gasped as the leather of my glove smashed into Shannon's jawbone, and for a moment I thought he might go down. Briggs hung on and I kept after him, but he got me with a hard hook just before the bell rang, ending the round.

We continued exchanging hard blows for twelve rounds, and nearly everyone in the arena thought that I was winning, far ahead on points—everyone except two of the three judges. During the final round the entire audience was on its feet, the crowd yelling and cheering us on. Blood was dripping from Shannon's nose as we exchanged strong punches in the center of the ring. Just before the final bell rang, Briggs let loose a flurry of punches and a lot of them landed. The fight ended with both of us standing and still swinging.

It seemed to take forever for the judges to tally their scores. When the decision was announced that Briggs had won, his cornermen jumped into the ring and lifted Shannon onto their shoulders as the crowd booed the verdict. Most fans, I later learned, had me winning eight or nine of the twelve rounds. Many thought that the fight had been rigged and that I had been robbed. I felt I had won the fight; the people believed I had won the fight. Even Shannon Briggs looked surprised that the judges declared him the winner. But the judges said that he had won, so I walked across the ring and congratulated the young boxer.

In the Good Book, I read about a time when King David, the second king of Israel, was discouraged, and even the people he had hoped to help were speaking evil of him. Distressed as he was, he decided that he would encourage himself and exercise his faith in God.[1] Sometimes that is exactly what you have to do. Don't wait around for everyone else to pat you on the back or tell you how talented you are; pat yourself on the back, and remind yourself of all the good things you have going for you.

Anyone can be encouraged when things are going well, when you are winning at every point. That's easy. But when you get knocked down on the canvas of life, that's the time to encourage yourself. Get up and remind yourself, *This is a new opportunity; my best days are ahead; this is going to be the best time of my life; my business and career are going to flourish.* What happened yesterday is over and done. You really can't do anything about what has happened in your past, but you can do a lot about your *attitude* regarding the past. Now is the time to seek the next opportunity.

Of course, I was discouraged and disappointed to hear the referee's voice reverberating throughout the arena, "And the winner is . . ." and he didn't call out my name. Nobody wants to lose, least of all me! For a few moments I had my own personal pity party. I wanted to dive under the canvas and escape the millions of eyes watching me. But that boxing match was history. Other people might want to talk about it for a long time, but that wasn't going to do me any good.

While I was still in the ring after the fight, the crowd was booing because the people felt that I had received an unfair decision. Home Box Office (HBO) fight commentator Larry Merchant pulled me close to his microphone and said, "Well, George, what do you say?"

"Have you ever heard of the George Foreman Lean, Mean, Fat-Reducing Grilling Machine?" I asked him. "Look at me," I gushed. "The grill works!" I shouted.

Larry looked shocked. "What does that have to do with the boxing match?" he asked.

"Nothin'," I said, "but you gotta talk about how good I feel. The grill works!" I looked straight into the camera and said, "No home should be without this thing." I smiled. "God bless you. Go get one!" The way I figured, I had a microphone in front of me, and this was my chance to make something good out of a bad situation.

The broadcaster continued to probe. "George, what are you going to do now?"

What an open door! I went on to tell him more about my new venture with the grill, and I turned that defeat into a new opportunity. To this day, people still come up to me and comment on my demeanor and sales pitch after that boxing match. Most of them can't remember who won the fight, but they know I didn't lose!

At the press conference after the Briggs fight, a lot of reporters asked me if I was going to give up boxing at last. "I don't think I'll be boxing again," I told them. "I don't need that anymore. I had fun tonight. There were a lot of boos and a lot of cheers, but all in all, I had a great time." Truth is, I was kind of glad to be out of that fight. Rather than respond to any more questions about my past, I immediately looked to the future. I knew I'd be busy promoting the grill.

One reporter asked me, "George, you lost this fight. Do you feel like you have been robbed?"

"Where I come from, when they rob ya, you don't have a pocket full of money," I quipped. Instead of feeling robbed, I felt incredibly blessed. The George Foreman grill was on the market, and I had done my best to promote it. Now I could only hope that the public would buy it.

And people really did. Men and women, college students and gourmet cooks, people everywhere bought the George Foreman grill, used it, and loved it. Just as important, they told their friends about it. My first royalty check for the grill was about $3,000; the next one was less, about $2,500. Then the next one was for more than $1 million! The next month's check was for $2 million, then $3 million! It got to the point where I was receiving royalties of nearly $5 million per month! The George Foreman grill became the single best-selling electrical appliance in history. When one dream dies or comes to an end, don't wallow in despair. Dream a new dream and then work hard to see it come to pass. That's what I did. I took every opportunity to promote the grill—doing interviews and television programs, constantly looking for a chance to turn the conversation from boxing to grilling—and it worked!

FIND A NEED AND FILL IT

Filling a need is not merely good business; it is a basic attitude toward life. If you see a need, do whatever you can to meet that need. If there is a piece of paper on the floor, rather than say, "That's not my job," bend over and pick it up! If the bed needs to be made, make it. If the car needs an oil change, instead of saying, "Well, my spouse will take care of that," take the car to the auto service garage and have the work done. If the copier at work needs paper, don't call for a technician (unless that is your company's policy), just fill the machine with paper. Although this seems simple, you'd be amazed how many people will say, "Well, that is not my responsibility." But people who are successful in life see the world as their responsibility. The attitude of "What can I do to help?" will take you much further than the attitude of "What tasks can I avoid?"

The secret to entrepreneurial success is doing something that fills a need—finding a quality product or service that is beneficial to a large segment of the public. Niche products are nice—after all, who couldn't use a crank-powered radio to prepare for future calamities? Novelty items are cute, but they rarely bring long-term success. On the other hand, if you have a quality product or service that is beneficial to a broad segment of society—something that everybody needs or wants, or people can use in various cultures—you will find a market, or the market will find you.

In your business or career pursuits, you must find something that you believe in—a goal you would pursue even if you never made a dime at it. You have to look beyond where you are today and see where you want to be in the future. Don't limit yourself by the current situation; instead consider the potential for success. Having a good product or service isn't enough if you don't believe in it. On the other hand, once you find something you believe in, something you know will be helpful to other people, you will be over the toughest hurdle on your way to success. Determine to learn everything you can about the business or career you have chosen. Attempt to become an expert in your field, and aim at becoming the best at what you do. You never stop working at something you truly believe in. When I first decided to become a professional boxer, I not only trained my body but also my mind. I studied old films of champion boxers, noticing their styles, looking for keys to their success. And then I tried to incorporate what I'd learned into my own circumstances, given my size, weight, and speed. I studied even more when I made a second run at the championship. I knew I couldn't simply overpower my competition; I had to outthink them as well.

MONEY MATTERS, BUT NOT MUCH

Don't let making money be your only motivation. I know it may be difficult to believe, but money is not the best motivator for most people. If you find a product or service that will simply make money for you, you can pay the mortgage this month, but that will never be enough to motivate you to outstanding success. You must look beyond money to something about which you can be passionate, something that will not only motivate you in the short term but also sustain you over the long haul. Rather than focus on the mere accumulation of money, aspire to achieve satisfaction and significance.

Lasting significance can be measured by how helpful you are to other people. And money will come if you have something to offer; in fact, you will probably receive more money in direct proportion to how helpful you can make yourself to other people. Don't let anyone fool you into believing that you are selfish for wanting to do something significant. It's just the opposite. There is something noble about going to work each day, so always keep in mind that what you are doing matters. You are a great person for providing a product or service the world wants or needs, and the world will reward you accordingly. Be sincere, make sure you have a product or service that is beneficial, and when the opportunity comes for you to talk about it, tell the truth. People will respond to your honesty and sincerity, and your passion for the product or service will be contagious. Before long you will notice an increase in the size of your wallet. As the old saying goes, "Do something you love, and the money will follow."

Do your homework. Pitch only a top-quality product or service. Few people do well at a career that deep down they feel is a sham or is unworthy of their best efforts. Timing is important too. Sometimes a plan or a product is ahead of its time and takes awhile to catch on. Be patient, but keep your eyes on the marketplace. If there is no demand for the product, plan, or service you are providing, then you must either create the demand or find a new career.

You cannot pretend when it comes to this matter of success. Certainly you shouldn't measure your progress in dollars and cents alone, but don't be so naïve that you think money doesn't matter at all. If you are not moving forward measurably in your career, and you are not making a living by doing what you are doing, it is time for a change. For example, if you are working at a job that you hate or for which you feel you don't have the skills required and you can't readily obtain them, that is a major indicator that you need to do something else. If you can't do your work wholeheartedly, the best half-hearted effort will never satisfy you. Nor will it satisfy your employers. On the other hand, many people leave their jobs too soon; they launch out into some entrepreneurial effort prematurely. Then they get discouraged when success seems elusive. You must be realistic. I'll say more about failure being an important part of success in chapter 11, but for now, please know that money is not the key indicator. You should ask yourself whether you are experiencing a good measure of satisfaction and significance in what you are doing. If not, a career change may be the answer.

GET OFF THE TREADMILL

I'm convinced that owning your own business—designing your own plan and controlling as many of the variables as possible—is one of the best ways to become successful today. Obviously, most of us work for someone else at some point in our careers. I had several one-stop jobs in my younger years, and I've had a few dead-end jobs as an adult. But don't limit yourself to what you can earn by working for someone else.

While you may be an excellent worker at a nine-to-five job, most truly successful people I know spend far more than eight hours a day working at something they love. Similarly, while you may earn increasingly better wages or salaries as you advance in your career, and may make wise choices in saving and investing your money, most people who obtain the greatest satisfaction and get fabulously wealthy in the process are not hourly work-ers. No, they *own* the businesses that employ the hourly workers. Even if you must start your business while working for someone else, work hard at it, set high goals for yourself, and persevere no matter what obstacles are in your way. You will love the freedom that comes from being your own boss. Certainly along with that freedom come responsibilities of a different sort: as your own boss, you also get to manage the many details involved in running your own business, from dealing with employee issues to paperwork and taxes. But the pluses of owning your own business far overshadow the minuses.

"That sounds great, George," I hear you saying, "but I barely have time to make ends meet now with my responsibilities at work, my children, my spouse, and my other commitments. There's no way I can start my own business right now."

Okay, maybe you can't take on any new responsibilities at this juncture in your life, but make it a goal to work toward being your own boss. If you can't own your own business, develop a skill or refine a talent that makes you extremely valuable to someone who does own his or her own business. You will always be in demand if you can do something or offer skills that others cannot.

Building a successful career from scratch takes courage, but it is also tremendously exciting. When you start at the bottom and work your way up, you appreciate success when you get there. In the meantime, it is always an adventure. Sometimes you can almost feel the electricity in the air because you know you are working for yourself rather than the boss or the company.

I heard a story about a man who owned his own farm. Back in the days before tractors came with headlights already installed, the farmer figured out a way to rig up floodlights on his tractor so he could work after sundown. You have to wonder, would he have had that same drive and competitiveness that spawned ingenuity and greater production if he had been working for another landowner rather than himself?

WE'RE ALL IN BUSINESS

As an entrepreneur, you are working for yourself. You are calling your own shots, determining your destiny. Truth is, even if someone else signs your paycheck, you are still in business for yourself. We all are!

A young farm boy from northern Illinois discovered this truth early in the twentieth century. He moved to Chicago, hoping to find a job and develop a career in the big city, but all he could find was a job as a clerk in a drugstore on Chicago's South Side. The young man worked hard, but his boss was a real taskmaster who didn't seem to appreciate him, so he decided to quit and look for something else. But almost on a whim, he thought, *I'm going to quit, but before I do, I'm going to make my boss sorry to lose me.*

He worked even harder at doing the best job he could, even though his boss remained ungrateful. Although the boss didn't notice, somebody else did—the drugstore owner—and the owner gave the young clerk a raise. The young man took it as a personal challenge and continued his efforts to do excellent work, determined to make his presence missed when he finally walked out the door for the last time. Before long, however, he received another raise, so he decided to stay at the job awhile longer. Meanwhile, during the evening hours when things were slow, the young man studied more and more about pharmaceuticals and what it took to run a pharmacy.

In 1901, he purchased his own drugstore, a small neighborhood store on the South Side. The store was rather ordinary; it looked and operated pretty much like all the other drugstores in the city. The young man, however, decided to do business differently. He enjoyed helping his customers, and he let it show in his face and in his attitude. He told his few employees, "If the customers feel important, they will come back." And they did.

Slowly but surely, he built a reputation for good customer service. The young pharmacist employed one of his favorite customer service techniques when a customer phoned in an order to be delivered. (Back in those days, doctors made house calls and pharmacists made deliveries.) While he talked with the person on the phone, he would signal a helper and repeat the order, loud and clear, while filling the prescription. Then, while he continued to talk with the customer, engaging in casual conversation, the helper packaged the order and hustled out the door to his bicycle. Sometimes if the customer lived close enough, a knock on the door would interrupt the pharmacist and the customer's phone conversation. Upon answering the door, the customer would be surprised to find the pharmacist's helper standing there with the order.

The young pharmacist used such techniques to build a reputation for small-town customer service even in the big city. His enthusiasm was contagious. Soon he opened a second store, then a third. Eventually his stores became one of the largest drugstore chains in the United States, and you can probably find one on a corner near you. That young pharmacist who was willing to do a little more than most was Charles R. Walgreen Sr., founder of Walgreens.

Similarly, when consumers began to think more ecologically and the need for more environmentally safe cleaning products became obvious, my son George III and I immediately launched the Knock-Out Pro Green cleaning products. We already had a line of cleaning products based on natural cleaning agents that didn't contain ammonia or alcohol. For instance, we had George Foreman's Knock-Out Multi-Purpose Cleaner, which included a deep stain remover, a glass cleaner, and other home and industrial cleaning agents. But as we learned more about the need for environmentally safe products, we began retooling our line to be even more ecologically sound. We found a need that we could meet, and we found ways of doing it better than most other companies.

Recognizing a need also led me to the restaurant business. As anyone who has ever traveled knows, it is extremely difficult to find a fast, reasonably priced, nutritious meal in America's airports or along our highways. Many fast foods are not all that good for you. So, along with the UFood Restaurant Group, my company, George Foreman Enterprises, set out to develop a chain of fast-casual restaurants and nutritional product retail stores. As I write these words, it is too early to tell what our bottom line will be, but I am convinced that with Americans wanting and needing to eat more nutritionally, we will be meeting a need long ignored by other restaurateurs. A number of my celebrity friends have been involved in restaurants that went broke. Why? Because they didn't meet a need and the food was often overpriced or less than the best quality. If you want people to spend their hard-earned cash, you better provide them with a good product.

Finding a need and filling it is a key principle for a Knockout Entrepreneur. Your chances of being successful increase exponentially if you not only find a need and fill it, but also can do it better than anyone else. That's what Fred did.

Fred Smith was a twenty-eight-year-old Vietnam vet, honorably discharged from military service. In 1973, he ran a family-owned aviation maintenance company in Little Rock, Arkansas, but he was continually frustrated when parts he needed didn't show up until four or five days after the shipper had sent them out.

Fred realized that much of the problem was due to the unreliability of the commercial airlines that transported packages and air freight in their cargo hulls. Asking around, Fred discovered that he was not the only consumer dealing with the annoying inconvenience and being at the mercy of the big airlines. He began thinking of a small-package delivery service to meet that need.

Risking his entire family inheritance, Fred purchased a couple of small jets and began Federal Express, a company more commonly known today as FedEx. Fred's intention was to provide a service that could deliver parcels that "absolutely, positively had to be there" overnight, a concept that became a major part of his early marketing and advertising slogans.

Many people tried to discourage Fred, telling him that his idea would never work. The first night Fred's Falcon Jet made its initial runs, Fred wasn't so sure either. He had only six packages to deliver, and one of those was a birthday gift he was sending to a friend. But Fred's fledgling company delivered the packages overnight and on time. His idea soon caught on, and FedEx created an entirely new service industry, changing the way America does business and developing into a multibillion-dollar overnight delivery service. The company is so firmly established as an overnight package deliverer of choice that many people use *FedEx* as a verb: "I'll FedEx it to you tomorrow."

BE WILLING TO BREAK WITH THE STATUS QUO

Sometimes doing things better means doing things *differently* than they've been done before. If you have lived in America within the past seventy-five years, you have probably had a vacuum cleaner in your home. My mom used a broom to clean our house, and she wasn't bashful about using that broom on me too when I got out of line, but that's another story.

One day a fellow named James Dyson was vacuuming his home, and he noticed that after a few minutes, his sweeper began to lose some of its suction, doing a good job on part of the carpet, but missing other dust, fabric, or small pieces of paper. He also noticed that the bag and filter on the vacuum frequently clogged, reducing the suction and effectiveness of the vacuum. He had to keep going back over the same areas, adding up to more work.

James Dyson set out to solve the problem, but he didn't want to do the same old thing in the same old way that vacuum manufacturers had always done. He hoped to eliminate the need for vacuum cleaner bags altogether and design a vacuum cleaner that didn't lose suction. He believed that if he could develop a vacuum cleaner that did a better job more quickly and more efficiently, even if it cost more, people would buy it.

Dyson persevered in his project. It took him several years and more than five thousand prototypes before he finally perfected a machine that required no bags and maintained its suction. But when James Dyson took his new invention to major manufacturers of vacuum cleaners, one by one they turned him down. They preferred selling vacuums with bags because they were making more than $500 million a year restocking bags for existing vacuum cleaners.

Finally Dyson's vacuum cleaner, known as the G-Force with its cyclone technology, was introduced at the International Design Fair in Japan, a premier trade show for the latest high-tech products. Dyson won first prize with his vacuum cleaner. The Japanese were so impressed with the G-Force that it became a status symbol in their homes, selling for as much as two thousand dollars each.

James Dyson returned home and decided to use the money he had received from the Japanese license to develop a new model he could market under his own name. He encountered one difficulty after another and came dangerously close to going bankrupt during the years it took to develop his high-end vacuum cleaner. Some people thought that Dyson was crazy, that the public would never pay that much to suck up household dust. But James Dyson believed he could make a better product that people would want to buy—and he did.

Today more than fifteen million Dyson vacuum cleaners are in homes all over the world, many with a retail sales price of nearly five hundred dollars each. Dyson's original team of three engineers has grown to hundreds of scientists and engineers, searching for ways to make everyday products work better. James Dyson not only found a need and filled it, but he created a need for bagless vacuum cleaners and pioneered it.

YOU MUST SEE IT BEFORE YOU CAN BE IT

If you hope to enjoy long-term success, you must first believe that you can do it. Do you remember the classic line from the children's story *The Little Engine That Could*? "I think I can. I think I can." That little train's passionately felt belief came true. On the other hand, if you think you are unable to succeed, you are predicting your own failure.

As a Knockout Entrepreneur, you must see yourself winning, see yourself earning enough money to live the way you want to live, see yourself being promoted at work, see yourself taking your product to people and bettering their lives as a result. See yourself winning the award, receiving the big contract, and being able to help other people on a scale you've only dreamed about till now. Imagine that bright and optimistic future, and then learn how to share that vision with others; work at energizing and motivating people to turn those dreams into realities.

I believe it helps to write down specific, tangible, realistic dreams and goals you have for your business or career before you even make up a business card. Rather than saying simply, "I want a better job," define what that means for you. What kind of job, doing what kind of work? Do you need more training or education to secure that kind of work? If so, where and when will you start to get it? Be specific. If you are working too hard and know that you need to take a vacation, don't simply say, "Next year I plan to work less and enjoy life more." That's great, but what are you going to do differently? When and where will you take that vacation? How much will it cost? How much do you need to be saving each week to make that vacation a reality? When you start writing down the specific targets at which you are aiming, you'll be amazed at how many more you hit.

From day one, keep that vision in focus, and know where you want to go and how you plan to get there. Having a plan and a vision statement—a simple sentence or two describing what you plan to do, how, and why—will help you sort out what is important for your business. It will also help you avoid getting involved in things that don't matter or at least don't have significant reason to be on your priority list. As the old saying goes, "If you don't know where you are going, then it doesn't matter which direction you go." With a good road map or a game plan, you will have a much better chance of becoming a Knockout Entrepreneur.

Open your eyes and see the opportunities all around you. Remember, you can't simply see things as they are; if you want to be successful, you must see them as they can be. If you will find or develop a product that is beneficial to others or a service that meets a need in some way that others cannot, you will discover the market or the market will discover you. And you will be on your way to becoming a Knockout Entrepreneur!

KNOCKOUT IDEAS
TO STIMULATE YOUR SUCCESS

1. Have you ever had an idea for a new product or service, or maybe a career move, but you didn't act on it? Then six months later you saw something similar on the market or learned that someone else had made that move and it was hailed as a brilliant, much needed idea. What limited you or held you back from pursuing your dream?

2. What will you do differently the next time an opportunity opens to you?

3. Look around your workplace and notice the areas that are not operating at full potential. What could you do to improve that situation? What need can you fill better than anyone else there? Remember, you will be paid according to how helpful you are to other people.

CHAPTER TWO

LISTEN TO YOUR CORNER

M ost people don't think of boxing as a team sport; they see it as one boxer pitted against another. But if that's your perception, you are missing a key element of any great fighter's success—the team around the person in the ring.

The most important individuals on a boxer's team are the cornermen. Every successful boxer has at least three people in his corner, helping him be his best. First is his trainer, who has worked with him on the road for months, carefully tracking his breathing, strength, and energy levels. During the heat of a battle, a boxer may not be the best judge when it comes to assessing how well he is holding up, what strategic steps he needs to take, or what changes he can make. Sometimes he needs to hear the objective voice of the trainer saying, "Slow down. Pace yourself. Conserve your energy." Or sometimes the trainer can challenge or encourage the boxer to take risks, letting him know that he has a deep reservoir to draw from, so he doesn't need to fear expending too much energy. "Go for it! Don't hold back," he might prod the boxer.

Another key person in the boxer's corner is the technician, the trainer's scout, so to speak. He knows what the opposition is doing and where the weak spots in the competition can be found. Of course, he should be courageous enough to speak straightforwardly about your weak points too, and how you can best compensate for them. He may say something like, "Keep your hands up; you're dropping your hands and giving the opposition an open shot." At the same time he must be honest with you, especially about the tactics that will succeed and the tactics that are a waste of time and energy, realistically helping you to discover and use your best qualities that will work most effectively for you against the current competition.

The third key individual in the corner is the cut man. His job is to patch up any problems, to take care of minor injuries, making sure a small cut doesn't turn into an open gash. He doesn't have to say a word; he just needs to keep his focus, looking for trouble spots or areas of swelling or potential bleeding. He then moves quickly and efficiently to prevent new problems from occurring while taking care of those areas where the fighter is vulnerable to further injury.

You should have a strong team of people around you as well, even if you are self-employed. In most cases, achieving your success will be a team sport, and just as it takes a good group effort to make a successful championship boxer, your success in business and in life will be greatly enhanced by getting good people in your corner and learning to trust them so completely that when times get tough, you know you can count on their wisdom and advice.

You need a trainer, a visionary, someone who will help you see beyond yourself. Visionaries are people who will dream with you about what can be, rather than merely talk about the good old days or even the present days.

Your visionary might be a mentor, a pastor, or a good friend who believes in you and is willing to shoot straight with you. Or perhaps your visionary is your spouse or a member of your board of directors. Keep in mind that your spouse, friend, or board member may love or admire you so much that their advice can be skewed by their emotions. You may need to balance their opinions with a person who has a more objective perspective. Whoever your visionary is, you must give that person permission to speak truth to you, even when it hurts, and to help you expand your horizons and set your sights on higher goals.

You should also have a good accountant in your corner. The accountant is your technician, someone who keeps her eyes on the opposition and scouts out the competition. This person really understands the intricacies of the tax laws and is willing to help you maximize your business or personal income by taking advantage of every legal expense or deduction.

Don't mess with shysters. You know the type: the tax guy who tells you that you don't need to pay taxes because the dollar does not really have any value anymore, that there is no gold or silver standing behind American money, so you are receiving nothing but a piece of paper in which you place your trust; therefore you don't owe the government any taxes. That's a bunch of malarkey, but people out there are peddling that stuff every year, and every year somebody else gets in big trouble. I'm not an accountant— although I do have a good one on my team—but I can tell you this much: no matter whether you get paid in dog bones or sweet potatoes, you are liable for taxes on your earnings in this great country. As a matter of personal integrity, don't try to evade paying taxes.

Understand, it is legal to *avoid* paying any more than necessary, and that is a wise financial choice, so find the best accountant you can. Just make sure he knows you want everything done on the up-and-up—no compromises, no shady deductions, no expenses that cannot be substantiated. Then pay what you owe, and keep a smile on your face. Be thankful that you live in a country where your income is limited only by your willingness to work hard and use your entrepreneurial talents.

A story in the Bible illustrates this principle. When a few Pharisees tried to trap Jesus into either alienating some Jewish people or recommending that people not pay taxes to Rome, Jesus asked for a coin. When He was presented a Roman coin, Jesus asked, "Whose image is on this coin?"

The image was that of Caesar, the Pharisees replied.

Jesus told them straightforwardly, "Then render to Caesar the things that are Caesar's, and render to God the things that are God's."

In other words, we pay our taxes because the government has a right to tax us for the benefits we receive and for the common good of our nation, but our lives belong to God. As such, out of personal integrity and commitment to God, we should willingly pay our fair share. But that doesn't mean that you need to pay more tax than is required. And that's where having a good accountant in your corner can help you.

Your technician needs to be especially honest about your tactics. In boxing, the technician has to have enough courage to tell you that your jab is too slow and it isn't working against the opposition, or that your opponent is beating you in some other way. This is even more difficult as you rise in the ranks of your career and people start telling you how smart you are, how skilled you are, or in general what an amazing person you are. You will be tempted to start believing your own press releases. That's why you need someone who can cut through all that and say, "Champ, here's what you need to do if you want to win." It takes courage to tell someone who thinks he's the best that there is a way he can be better. You will be blessed to have someone who is not only honest but also technically correct about your tactics, helping you to make the right moves that will lead you to success.

In addition to the visionary and the accountant, you should have a good lawyer in your corner—your personal cut man—someone who can patch you up when you take a hard shot. Your cut man should be willing to ask you the difficult questions about your business, including your ethics. This person will shoot straight with you and not simply tell you what you want to hear. These three cornerpeople will be as vital to your success as my cornermen were to my boxing success.

KEEP INTEGRITY FIRST

In business, you can never have too many friends. But the people in your corner—the ones you will listen to in the crunch times as well as the good times—should be people of integrity. Technical qualifications are important, but a highly qualified person who cheats will pull you and your entire team down. Even though he may bring certain talents and abilities to the table, that person's contributions are not worth it. Sooner or later, a talented person who lacks integrity will cost you much more than he has profited you. You dare not tolerate dishonesty in your corner.

On the other hand, you may find someone who is incredibly talented, but is not the kind of person with whom you enjoy spending time. The person may be the last person on earth you'd want to be friends with or with whom you'd want to hang out. Maybe he doesn't laugh at your jokes or doesn't dress the way you like. Maybe she prefers sushi to fried chicken. Be careful. Ask yourself, *Does this person have integrity? Can I trust her to tell me the truth? Can I trust her to do the right thing even when it hurts?*

If you find that the person has top-notch ability and personal integrity, even if he is not your favorite type of personality, you'd be wise to bring that person onto your team. Don't be afraid to employ people who will force you out of your comfort zone. Surround yourself with highly competent men and women of integrity and your success is almost guaranteed. Surround yourself with highly competent people who are willing to compromise their personal integrity and, sooner or later, their tendency to lower the standards will take a toll on you and your business as well.

CHOOSE *COMPETENT* PEOPLE FOR YOUR CORNER

Most fighters choose cornerpeople they like, friends or family members who may not always be the most qualified to do the best job for the boxer. Early in his career, an amateur often teams up with a particular cornerman because of convenience, friendship, or finances. That's understandable. But then as the amateur turns professional, he tends to take his cornerman along with him as he moves up the rungs on the ladder of success. That cornerman may not be the best person for you as you grow and may not bring out the best in you. In times of adversity, or as the competition stiffens, he won't be able to help you. Certainly you should be loyal to the people who have helped you along the way, but if you want to keep advancing, you must find the best, most qualified people and get them in your corner.

At the peak of Mike Tyson's career, he had Jimmy Jacob in his corner. Jimmy was the consummate cornerman. When I first met Jimmy, he was buying up all sorts of boxing films—old fights of champion boxers—and studying them. I was just starting out, so I often went over to his place to watch films with him. We studied films of Joe Louis, Jack Dempsey, and so many others, and I learned by watching their moves. My trainer and manager at the time, Dick Sadler, thought that Jimmy was trying to steal me away from him, so he squawked about me spending so much time watching films with Jimmy. But Dick didn't understand that Jimmy was helping me.

"Come on, let's get out of here," he said brusquely when he found Jimmy and me watching films. "That's enough of that. We gotta go."

Dick's jealous attitude offended Jimmy. He said, "One day I'll have a fighter of my own, and I'll teach him how to be the best." And of course, he did. He took Mike Tyson from obscurity to the top of the boxing world.

Unfortunately, after Jimmy Jacob passed away, Mike didn't replace him with a qualified head cornerman. One of the reasons Mike Tyson lost his fight to Buster Douglas was that he had people in his corner who were not highly competent. He had hired his buddies to work in his corner, his friends rather than people who knew what they were doing and were able and willing to help Mike be his best.

When I prepared to box Evander Holyfield, I did something similar. I had Charlie Shipes in my corner. Charlie was a good trainer, but he was not a great cornerman. He was a good friend, and he'd get excited when things were going well and overly concerned if they were not. Consequently his decisions weren't always as objective as they needed to be. I loved Charlie, and he may have worked out well for other fighters, but I shouldn't have put him in a position where our friendship colored his ability to make the tough calls.

At the same time I had Archie Moore in my corner, another good man and a good friend. He was a former world light heavyweight champion who had boxed well into his fifties. He had also trained a young guy named Cassius Clay before he turned professional and later changed his name to Muhammad Ali. He was a great teacher and a fine technician, but not a great cornerman. When we started training for a fight, I'd hire a good cut man, and he was often my best advocate in the corner.

I kept Charlie and Archie with me because I trusted them as individuals, but I didn't rely on their fight expertise as much as I would have. That was my fault, not theirs.

In the same manner, if you keep unqualified or ill-prepared men or women on your staff even though they are not doing the best job, that's your fault, not theirs. They are just making a living; you are forging a career. You are not doing them or yourself any favors by keeping them in a no-win situation.

HAVE THE COURAGE TO TELL THE TRUTH

To succeed in boxing or in business, you need somebody in your corner who cares enough to challenge you and is courageous enough to tell you the truth, especially when the pressure is on. During my infamous 1974 "Rumble in the Jungle" fight in Zaire against Muhammad Ali that later came to be known as the "Rope a Dope" fight,[1] I could feel Ali starting to relax. It was obvious that he thought he was the tough guy who had me on the run. *That's good*, I thought. *I'm going to lull him into complacency, and then I'm going to nail him.*

Just about that time, I heard Ali's cornerman, Angelo Dundee, calling out to him, "Muhammad, don't play with that sucker!" Ali turned up the heat, and I ended up losing that bout. But I never forgot the turning point, when Dundee had the right word at the right time.

I later said to myself, *If there is ever a chance to get Angelo Dundee in my corner, I want to do it.*

Too often in business, we surround ourselves with yes-people, people who will agree with the boss on almost everything. But if you are going to advance in business or be successful at anything in life, you need people around you who love you enough (or at least are honest enough) to tell you the truth, people with the courage to look you in the eye and say, "I don't think that is the best move for you right now" or "I know that is what everybody else is doing, but that is not a good choice for you."

When I heard that Angelo Dundee might be available, I talked to boxing promoter Bob Arum and said, "I'd like to get Angelo to work with me. What do you think?"

"Well, he's expensive," Bob replied, "but he's the best. If you want the best, give him a call."

I had to lay aside my ego, a difficult thing for anyone to do, but especially for someone who believes he is one of the best boxers in the world. Keep in mind, too, that Angelo had called me a sucker, a term of derision. But I had to forget about my personal feelings; I had to get past the fact that Angelo had worked for Ali, and Ali had knocked me out, thanks to Angelo's advice. I had to forget about the embarrassment that incident had cost me and the fact that Angelo had already cost me millions of dollars in money I didn't make, thanks to my loss to Ali. I knew that, like me, Angelo Dundee was a pro. Boxing wasn't personal to him; he regarded boxing as strictly business. He was the best, and I wanted the best.

I called Angelo and we talked about the possibilities. He was more expensive than many other cornermen who would do an okay job. A good cornerman can do an adequate job, but a *great* cornerman can take you to the next level. So I agreed to pay Angelo the higher price.

Now I had a problem: in my corner I had two good friends and one expert. I have often wondered whether I might have been more successful with three top-quality experts in my corner.

Ironically, Angelo was never a superior fighter; he was more like a field general who knew how to best marshal his forces to win the battle. Yet in his own way, he knew how to motivate and bring out the best in a boxer. Some boxers, for instance, respond better to a rough approach—tough talk and swearing—but that wasn't going to work with me. Angelo found the best way to communicate with me was not a loud, bombastic approach, but a low-key, quiet word at the right time.

When I was forty-five years of age, the oldest man ever to box for the world heavyweight championship for the second time, I faced a tough young fighter named Michael Moorer. The fight was vicious, but I felt confident that I was delivering hard blows and that Moorer would eventually succumb. Angelo Dundee wasn't quite so sure. In the ninth round as I stood in my corner, Angelo looked me in the eyes and, with the crowd in the arena going wild, he spoke humbly and quietly to me: "You're doing good, George, but you might be behind on points. I don't know if you want to lose this match or not, but if you want to win, you better get this over."

I looked back at Angelo and said, "What are you bothering me for? I know exactly what I'm doing." I got so upset, I went back to the bout and knocked out Michael.

Angelo was worth every penny I paid him. He was with me in my corner during the most difficult times of my comeback career, and he helped me to do what no other human being had ever done—win the heavyweight boxing championship of the world at forty-five years of age. Angelo and I didn't always see eye-to-eye, but he was courageous enough to tell me the truth, and I needed a man like that in my corner.

Angelo smiled all the way to the bank.

FIND PEOPLE WHO ARE FILLED WITH HOPE

Don't allow negative people into your corner. You know who they are; they are the people whose vocabularies are filled with down words. They tend to talk about obstacles, complications, troubles, roadblocks, difficulties, frustrations, and failures rather than solutions, opportunities, goals, achievements, optimism, hopes, and dreams. Avoid input from negative people in general, but especially do not tolerate negative people in your corner. Instead, find people who believe in you and who want to rise with you to the top. Don't be satisfied with people in your corner who say, "This is my job." You want people who will say, "This is my chance! This is my chance to make something of my life; this is my chance to do something significant; this is my chance to improve; this is my chance to help somebody else fulfill his or her dreams."

Risk and uncertainty are parts of any business or career. But when a company spends the time and effort to sink a drill hundreds of feet into the ground in search of oil, the people responsible hope they will come up with a gusher! They may drill dozens of times and come up dry, but they continue to hope. They make the necessary adjustments and changes, but they never lose their hope of success. Certainly the oil company does not drill just anywhere or haphazardly. That would be silly. No, they have experience on their side. They study all the relevant information and get expert opinions on the circumstances. But their success is still grounded in hope. Hope takes courage and hope often involves work, but courage and work are useless without hope.

I like to stop by the George Foreman Youth and Community Center in Houston and watch some of the young people work out. I try to encourage each person, whether he or she possesses athletic ability or not. Occasionally I meet a young boxer who is working out as if he is going to be the next champion of the world. Why does he do that? Because he is filled with hope.

Wherever I go, I encourage people to dream bigger, to hope for better. Some people are so trapped by their past experiences or their present environment that they need somebody to tell them, "You can do more; you're better than that! You can dare to dream even bigger!" Basically I'm just giving them permission to do what they genuinely want to do anyhow, but for one reason or another, they have allowed themselves to become stifled and stunted in their dreams.

So let me tell you to dream bigger! You have my encouragement and permission to aim higher, do more, be more, earn more, and go further. If nobody else believes you can do it, I believe you can! Go after your dream and pour your life into reaching that goal. But whatever you do, commit to doing it with all your heart and don't stop until you get where you want to go.

REALIZE THAT YOU CAN NEVER HAVE TOO MANY PEOPLE IN YOUR CORNER

When I was preparing for a fight, I always had a number of assistants in training camp. Each one had specific responsibilities, and I could trust each one to get the job done right every time.

My son George III was my main flexibility trainer, helping me to stretch. I could have had a professional flexibility trainer, but I enjoyed having my son work with me. Even more important at the time, I didn't want anyone to know just how stiff and sore my body was; nobody knew my lack of flexibility except my son. It was just a game to him—he was helping Dad, even though Dad was yelping like a whipped pup, "Ouch . . . oooh, that hurts!"

George was also my encourager as I began running again. He was a relatively new driver, so he enjoyed driving the car behind me as I ran. "Come on, Dad. Just a little farther," he'd say, sitting up tall in the driver's seat.

"Hmmph, easy for you to say," I'd gasp.

Building a team and inspiring others to excellence require leadership. If you are going to be successful and significant in your world, that leadership must start with you. Too many leaders think that to motivate great performers, they must crack the whip. Wrong. Great performers usually motivate themselves; it may take a little effort on your part to keep them inspired, but your main job as the leader will be to encourage the less-than-great performers and to show respect to every person on your team. Pat the people on the back who are leading the pack, while you reach a hand back to help those who might be stumbling a bit. Without that appreciation and respect for other people, true leadership becomes ineffective, if not impossible.

You want everybody on your team; no one is excluded from being successful, but you should delegate responsibility only to the winners. Sometimes you can convert subpar performers and teach them how to be winners. Often it is a matter of placing the right person in the right position. On a baseball team, most catchers are not good center fielders; it would be a mistake to fire the player because he can't run fast enough in the field when his true talents might be at home plate. To get the best results, you must have your people working in the areas where they are strongest or most talented. The key is to find out where your team members' gifts and abilities lie, and then help them use their talents for the good of the business. A wide array of personality tests is available to help you determine your team members' strongest points. But you don't need to be a psychologist to observe what activities or responsibilities appeal most to your team members. Try to place your associates in the positions where they can be most productive for the entire team.

SEEK ADVICE FROM PEOPLE
WHO HAVE BEEN WHERE YOU WANT TO GO

Anytime you plan to go on vacation to someplace you have never been, it is usually helpful to talk with someone who has visited that place and can tell you where the good restaurants are and what the best way is to get around, as well as what things to take with you and what things to avoid or beware of once you arrive. In the same way, a Knockout Entrepreneur needs a guide, a mentor on his team. A mentor need not be someone you follow around like a puppy dog, but a good mentor should be an encourager or someone you can count on for accurate information as well as ruggedly honest feedback regarding how well you are doing and what you can do better. It's not necessary to spend hours on end with a mentor; often a mentor is someone you can call on the phone for sound advice and wise counsel along the way.

A true mentor doesn't tell you what to do, but might say something like, "I once faced a similar situation, and here's how I resolved it." We all need people who will encourage us to be our best, who will pass along insights and experiences. Too often we have to make some of life's most important decisions when we are least prepared to make them. For instance, a sixteen- or seventeen-year-old high school student must now make choices about which college he plans to attend to further his career—a career he doesn't even have yet! In the same way, many young couples make decisions about getting married, buying a home, having children—all of which are life-changing decisions—based on little to no experience. That's why the younger you are, the more you need a mentor.

Mentoring is not merely instructing; it involves having a relationship built on trust, in which your mentor coaches and encourages you. She may inspire you to attempt something you ordinarily would be reluctant to try. Or he may provide special knowledge about your field that you could not find anywhere else or that might be difficult for you to learn on your own. Strangely enough, although we live in a world inundated with information on how to do almost anything or how to do it better, most of us still tend to ask our family members, friends, neighbors, or coworkers for advice on important matters. We trust these people and value their opinions.

That's great if the people from whom we seek advice actually have expertise in the areas in which we need help. If they don't, they will normally reinforce what we *want* to hear rather than tell us what we *need* to hear. In their book *Driving the Career Highway*, authors Janice Reals Ellig and William J. Morin concur that the advice of those closest to you may often be skewed when it comes to your career. They write,

> Though you trust your close friends and family members, they can be the least effective of "counselors" when it comes to helping you think about your career. The reason is simple: because your friends and family members love you, they want you to be happy. Their tendency is to comfort you, to tell you that "things will work out all right" or that "you'll get over it." Although soothing, such advice is not particularly helpful. So think about consulting a professional. After all, you go to a professional physician when your health is at issue and to a professional accountant or financial planner for help in thinking through the state of your finances. Shouldn't you consider seeing a professional counselor when assessing and evaluating whether your career is taking you where you want it to go?[2]

That's why most successful people constantly seek guidance from experts in their field. Having a mentor is the ideal, but if you can't find one, at least listen to audio materials or read books by people you hope to emulate. Follow the clues to their success. Where they are applicable, try to incorporate those ideas into your life. Remember, every person is different and you will need to tailor the ideas and advice you receive to your individual talents and situations. You may not always experience the same results as the person offering nuggets of wisdom. That's okay. Keep growing; keep looking for ways that you can do what you do better. Seek advice that will help you define and clarify your goals and true desires, advice that will support you through your down times, fears, and insecurities and that will help you to do what you really need to do rather than just the minimum required.

AVOID CLONING YOURSELF

In most cases you don't need another you. Instead, gather people around you who have talents unlike yours or who can do what you can't or don't want to do.

Bill Gaither is one of the most prolific and successful songwriters in America. He and his wife, Gloria, have written more than seven hundred published songs and have won numerous awards for their music. In 2000, the American Society of Composers, Authors, and Publishers (ASCAP) honored Bill and Gloria as the Christian songwriters of the *century*! Not surprisingly, besides being a songwriter, Bill is a piano player and a singer. But for years the Gaithers have been performing to sold-out arenas around America and in various parts of the world, not because of Bill's great playing and singing ability, but because Bill has always had a knack for finding outstanding new talents and introducing them to his audiences. Although he is hugely successful and a true icon in his industry, Bill lays aside his ego and allows other performers to shine. The fans keep coming and the turnstiles keep turning. And everybody wins—the audiences hear new performers, the new talents find a built-in audience, and Bill is mighty happy too.

Nobody can do everything well, so learn how to delegate responsibility to other winners and then hold them accountable for their decisions. Have people around you who are smarter than you. We all need the expertise of other people, so make sure the people who represent you in the business world interact regularly with you. Learn how to rely on their skills and give them freedom to do what they do best, but don't give them so much freedom that they have no accountability. Make sure to have an evaluation system in place so everyone is aware of what is expected, and some way of telling when they aren't fulfilling those expectations.

I once lost money on a microfilm business (in the pre–desktop computer days) primarily because the manager didn't know what he was doing, but also because I wasn't paying enough attention to what he was doing. The product had my name on it, not his. Another problem was that the salespeople didn't believe in themselves. I went to numerous meetings, pitching our products to big companies and then going back to our company to teach them how to do the presentations. For some reason they grew dependent on me as the pitchman, pinning their success to my ability to see the presidents or decision makers of our potential clients. My manager and employees never caught the vision that they could make the company fly with or without me; that it was really up to them, not me. They didn't believe enough that we had a great product and that they could sell it.

To be successful, you may not always know what to do, but you must have people around you who do.

TAKE ACTION WHEN PEOPLE AREN'T LIVING UP TO THEIR POTENTIAL

Finding the right people with whom to work and avoiding the wrong people are essential to your success. If you surround yourself with negative thinkers and adopt the attitudes of the "can't do it" crowd, you will not achieve your goals in regard to success, happiness, or significance. On the other hand, if you hold up successful people as your models, the other team members will recognize the attitudes, work ethic, and expertise that you believe leads to success.

What should you do when people aren't living up to their potential? First and foremost, you must hold them accountable for their actions, words, and attitudes. Lay on the encouragement and praise, but also let them know that you expect them to improve, to do better next time. Holding people accountable—checking and double-checking to make sure they are doing what is right—is a caring thing to do for your coworkers, friends, and family members. You never help others by allowing them to get away with giving less than their best efforts.

You don't need to be mean or rude in reprimanding someone who is not living up to expectations. Let the person know that you are interested in her long-term success. Rather than alienate an employee who is not producing, train the person to use her gifts and talents effectively. Putting the right people in the right positions is a key factor to success. Remember, just because somebody has a degree in a subject doesn't necessarily qualify him for great success. A person may be related to you or may be a good friend, but if he is not an effective producer, find out what he is good at and move him into a position where he can flourish. If you cannot find a place where the person can contribute, you may have to let him go.

Recognize that you are probably not going to change that person in a few weeks or months. Adaptation and training may require a long process, and you will need to decide whether it is worth the effort. If not, you'd be better off to let that person go now.

Occasionally you may bring a person into your business who just doesn't seem to fit. She doesn't share your goals, values, ethics, work habits, or other qualities that you consider important. Or that person may be self-centered or show little interest in the welfare of the business. Or perhaps he is not a good example of the image you hope to project to the community. What should you do?

As much as I hate to say it, if that person's presence is pulling down the entire operation and you have honestly tried to help her find her niche in your business, then you as the boss or leader must act. You must admit that you made a mistake in bringing this person on board and that you are not doing that person or yourself any favors by prolonging the pain. Not everybody is meant to be a Knockout Entrepreneur, and if a person is not genuinely excited about being a part of your organization or group, you are doing her a disservice by retaining her. People lacking in passion for their work should most likely find some other occupation. Truly successful Knockout Entrepreneurs understand that their work is moral, noble, and worthwhile, and that gives them a tremendous competitive edge in the marketplace.

DON'T EVEN LISTEN TO NON-WINNERS

I don't like to view anyone as a loser, but the simple truth is, some people simply are not winners. They don't have a winning attitude; they aren't willing to pay the price to win; they are too quick to compromise their integrity or the integrity of the company or organization; worst of all, they don't see themselves as succeeding. Never listen to them. Keep talking about good things; don't let the negative attitude seep inside you. Don't let them put those "can't win," "never happen," "can't do it" thoughts and words into your mind. The non-winners are the last ones to work in the morning and the first ones to leave in the evening, and you dare not allow their attitudes or actions to rub off on you.

If you are on a cross-country airplane flight and seated next to this type of person, you either have to move to another seat or keep talking! The last thing you want to do is *listen* to losers. Talk over them if you must; don't be quiet for a moment because they'll cast their "loser spell" over you if you let them! Their attitude says you just can't win at what you want to do.

For instance, when I won the heavyweight championship of the world, I had people coming out of the floorboards telling me what I ought to do with my prize money. Some said to invest it wisely; others had their own self-interest at heart. The ones I had to watch out for the most were the non-winners. They said, "George, you're the champion of the world; you can make a lot of money. You ought to quit boxing and get yourself a trucking company."

Now there's nothing necessarily negative about owning or working for a trucking company, but that wasn't a positive winning step forward for me. *A trucking company?* No, I was feeding my dream of being the heavyweight champion of the world. But if you're not careful, after a while, you'll start considering it, then dwelling on that idea. Before long, you'll be shopping for trucks! Don't let that happen to you.

You are a winner. You are a Knockout Entrepreneur. You have to feed yourself good thoughts; keep the goal that you want to achieve in front of you. When I was training for my boxing matches, I kept telling myself, *I'm going to be the heavyweight champion of the world.* I refused to listen to anything that even hinted at negativity.

While I was preparing to fight Evander Holyfield for the championship, I was sitting next to a fellow one day, and for a long while he was really quiet. Then almost under his breath, he said, "Man, that Holyfield—he sure is tough."

He wasn't speaking negatively; he wasn't speaking untruths. I just didn't need to hear that "you can't win" attitude seeping through his words. Not if I was going to go into the ring with any hopes of winning.

Granted, you can't keep people from interjecting their "can't win" poison philosophy into you. But you can keep putting the positive antidote out there. I look for people who ask questions such as, "What can I do to make things better?" or "How can we improve our quality or our service?"

And remember, people can change if they really want to, but they have to want it. You can't change others; you can only encourage them to adopt winning attitudes and actions and to believe in themselves.

Rather than seek to eliminate people from your team, it's always better to convert them if possible. Nathaniel was a young man whom most people had written off as someone who was never going to succeed, but I refused to give up on him. Occasionally I'd see him at the George Foreman Youth and Community Center, and I'd always try to encourage him. He was a talented fellow, but he constantly had some excuse for why he was not able to succeed.

"George, I was intending to meet you this morning, but my clock didn't go off."

"I'll try to make it, George, but you know the traffic is bad that time of day."

"I really want to do what you are saying, George, but I've been so busy . . ."

One day I saw him, and Nathaniel immediately launched into all his excuses. I went over to him and put an arm around his shoulder. "Do you know how many times you just said *but*?" I asked him. "I want to do it, but. I was going to be here, but. I want to do better, but." I looked him in the eyes and said, "Why don't you change that?"

"What can I say? What can I do?" he asked sincerely.

"Simply say, 'I'll see you in the morning,' " I replied. "Then be here on time and ready to get to work."

Nathaniel took that word to heart, and he began showing up on time for our meetings. Slowly but surely, he began to change as I helped him understand how he could make his life more productive.

Everybody can change; everybody can become a winner; anybody who really wants to do so can enjoy success and significance.

DON'T FORGET YOUR FAMILY

It is important to have your family members on your team, of course, whether they are actively involved in your career or not. What good is it for you to become a success in the eyes of the world, but a failure at home? Or worse yet, all the money in the world won't keep you warm at night if you lose your family while earning your fortune. Make sure your family members buy into your dream; let them share your success. You also need someone to salve your wounds when things don't go well. Sometimes you need to share your pain, to honestly admit your fears or insecurities, and there is no better place to do that than within the context of your loving family. Oftentimes those people closest to you can encourage you to keep going when you don't think you can take another step.

Your team members need to know that you care for them as people, that you care for their families and for them as individuals. Take a sincere interest in them. When you ask how they are doing, wait for an answer. Lots of people say to me, "Hey, George! How are you doin'?" Most of them don't really want to know. But if you will take an interest in the people on your team, they will respond positively.

Get in the habit of using this little phrase: "Tell me about you." Everyone has a story, but so few people want to listen. You give a person a priceless gift when you give him or her your complete attention. Look the person in the eyes while talking. By doing so, you are conveying a message: "What you have to say is important to me. I want to hear you and understand."

If you will listen to your team members and sincerely seek to learn what makes them tick, they will perform wonders for you. Treat them fairly and compassionately, and they will be inspired to do their best for you. Love is a much greater motivator than fear. If your team members love you, they will do everything in their power to help you and to avoid letting you down or disappointing you.

Always do right by the people who work for you or with whom you work. They have placed their trust in you; they depend on you. Go above and beyond what is expected, especially when you have the opportunity to compliment them or to show appreciation. Saying, "Hey, you guys have really done a great job" or "I'm so proud of you" will inspire your team far more than money will. Don't forget, though, that bonuses or unexpected financial rewards can be great motivators too.

Make sure you can trust the people in your corner, and then listen carefully to their advice. You may not always agree with them and you may decide to move contrary to them at times, but at least you will have the honest feedback you need to make the best decisions possible. But always remember: the bottom line is yours. You can (and should) give your cornermen all the credit they deserve when you succeed, but when you fail, let the blame rest with you. Make sure you are well invested in a strong corner.

Of course, the best Person to have in your corner is the good Lord, but that's another book. Come to think of it, I already wrote that book.[3]

KNOCKOUT IDEAS
TO STIMULATE YOUR SUCCESS

1. Take a few moments to analyze your team. Who do you have in your corner? Are the people surrounding you qualified to speak words of wisdom or expertise into your life or business? Are they hard workers? Are they filled with hope?

2. Who are your closest associates? Are they lifting you up, energizing you, feeding you honest, truthful information, or are they dragging you down? The people with whom you spend the majority of your time will have an influence on how you think, act, and approach life.

CHAPTER THREE

NEVER LISTEN TO THE CROWD

My son George III ("Monk") was at home watching one of my boxing matches on television when he heard a person in the audience call out an extremely derogatory remark to me. "I just knew that Dad had to have heard that guy," Monk said, "because he was so loud and obnoxious. The remark hurt me as Dad's son, and I was sure it must have hurt Dad."

Later when Monk asked me about the nasty remark, I didn't even know what he was talking about. I hadn't heard the loudmouthed fellow. "I never listen to the crowd," I told Monk.

Many arenas in which I fought held twenty or thirty thousand people, but I could not allow myself to hear their voices, whether positive or negative. I concentrated on listening only to the men in my corner. Most professional athletes, whether boxers, tennis players, golfers, or baseball players, seek to put themselves in "a zone," a mental attitude where they are focused on only one thing: the challenge at hand. Thousands of people may be all around them, calling out their name, shouting admonitions or advice, but the focused athlete doesn't pay attention. He is in a zone.

In the same way, when it comes to your career or business, you cannot allow the crowd to influence you. In every crowd you will find some who cheer you on and others who jeer you and try to destroy your confidence. Don't pay attention to either group. Stay focused on the job at hand. You have the opportunity to do something great, so don't allow the squeaky wheels and the belligerent voices to distract you from what you know is important. By the same token, don't allow your cheerleaders to lull you into complacency or to cause you to become overconfident.

Usually the crowd doesn't have an accurate perception or a true understanding of the endeavor in which you are engaged. The crowd doesn't know the inside story or what you are really going through in the heat of the battle. Observers see who gets knocked down, who gets knocked out, or who wins or loses in the end. They fill everything else with empty and often false assumptions. A large percentage of the crowd doesn't even understand the real fight. If individuals in the crowd were that proficient in the principles involved in your business or craft, they'd be in the ring as fighters, trainers, managers, or consultants. But they are not; they are spectators, so don't allow them to influence your decisions. Remember, when the fight is over, whether the crowd has been cheering you on or booing you off the stage, the people will go home and on to the next diversion or entertaining activity. You, however, must make the best choices that will allow you to fight another day. You have to decide what is right for *you*.

I'll never forget watching Muhammad Ali boxing Larry Holmes.

Muhammad was getting beat, but he was not a quitter, so he stayed in the ring. The crowd was cheering him on, and even the guys in his corner were trying to pump him up, saying things like, "You can do it, Muhammad. You're the greatest. Get back in there and give it to him. Don't back off."

But Angelo Dundee, Ali's trainer at the time, knew better. He looked at Ali and said, "The fight is over."

The other guys in Muhammad's corner jumped up and protested. "You can't stop, Muhammad. You can't stop! Muhammad can still take him!"

Dundee stood up straight and said loud enough for Ali, the other cornermen, and the referee to hear, "Look, I'm the chief cornerman, and I say the fight is over."

That was it. Larry Holmes became the new heavyweight champion of the world.

When I saw Dundee's actions, I was impressed. I thought, *That is a brave man*. Dundee must have known that his decision was not going to be popular; he knew that it was going to cost his boxer and himself a lot of money. But he also knew when to say, "Enough is enough."

You need some people like that around you if you want to be successful in business and in life. Samuel Goldwyn, cofounder of the famous Metro-Goldwyn-Mayer Studios in Hollywood, was fond of saying, "I don't want any yes-men around me. I want everybody to tell me the truth even if it costs them their jobs."[1] Saying that it is time to pull the plug on one of your pet ideas will not make that person popular. It may cost both of you lots of time, energy, and money. But to continue down a road that is leading to destruction is foolish. You will be forever grateful to the man who says, "Stop, there's a bridge out up ahead."

Sometimes, of course, the crowd sees too small, with limited vision. The crowd may not realize that you have set your sights on a much loftier goal. For instance, when I first started on my boxing comeback, I'd meet people who would say, "You know, George, if you would just do this or that, you could make a million dollars."

I appreciated their concern for me, as well as their suggestions. But they had their sights set too low. I wasn't interested in making a million dollars. I was interested in earning a lot more than that because not only did I need to feed my family, I also wanted to bankroll the George Foreman Youth and Community Center in Houston, so I could help some kids get ahead in life. As fine a goal as a million dollars may be for someone else, it was too small a target for me. I saw no point in wasting my energy trying to convince those folks that my goal was to regain my title as heavyweight champion of the world. I just smiled and pursued my goal.

Once I met a fellow who claimed to be a boxing expert and wanted to give me advice about how I could improve. I was skeptical, but I was willing to talk with him. During the course of the conversation, he told me a story about another boxer who had been hit hard in the face. "He was hit so hard that he lost that teethus thing," the so-called expert said.

"Teethus thing?" I wasn't sure what he meant.

"Yeah, you know, that rubber thing you wear in your mouth when you're boxing."

"Oh, he lost his mouthpiece?" I asked.

"Yeah, he lost that teethus thing," the expert repeated.

"Well, it's been nice talking with you," I said. "Thanks for coming by." I figured if the man didn't know what to call a boxer's mouthpiece, he probably didn't know a better way to throw a left hook either.

Always be kind to the crowd, but never allow them to influence what you think or do for yourself. As a Knockout Entrepreneur, don't follow the crowd; let them follow you.

KNOCKOUT IDEAS
TO STIMULATE YOUR SUCCESS

1. Think of a time when the urgings of the crowd convinced you to do something that in your heart you did not want to do. How did you feel about yourself?

2. Learn to say, "Thanks, I appreciate that" or "That's an interesting idea" or some other noncommittal phrase when people who don't understand what you are trying to achieve offer their advice or opinions. You don't need to offend them, but you shouldn't waste your time listening to them either.

CHAPTER FOUR

MAKE IT GOOD

For most of my life, I've operated my businesses by a few simple truths: If it has your name on it, make it good, do it right, and always do more or better than is expected. Never promise more than you can deliver, but always deliver more than you promise. Your reputation as a person of excellence is one of your most valuable assets.

"But, George, why should I give the extra effort, providing more than I'm getting paid for or even noticed for?" you may protest. Truth is, if you go the extra mile and do more than necessary, eventually you will be paid more for what you do. But don't do it just for the money or recognition; do it because it is the best way to operate and the best way to build a reputation for excellence. Besides, when you have done more than what was required, given something extra, spoken more kindly than someone deserved, you will be amazed at how satisfied you feel at the end of the day. You'll feel good!

Before long, people will notice the quality of your work. They will know that if the proposal has your name on the cover, it is done right. If they buy a car from you, it will be clean and filled with gas when you deliver it to their home. Your reputation for making it good will bring you not only more clients but also customers who are willing to pay more to have things done right the first time. If clients want the best, they will call you or purchase your products.

I love it when I hear people say that they just purchased a new "George Foreman." What are they talking about? Most likely, they didn't purchase a George Foreman action figure or a George Foreman board game (hey, those aren't bad ideas!). Usually they are referring to the Lean, Mean, Fat-Reducing Grilling Machine—the George Foreman grill.

Other companies make portable grills. Our competitors are constantly trying to usurp our position as the best-selling electrical appliance in history. But the George Foreman grill has become so well known as the best product of its kind, and it is so familiar a brand to the public, that many people refer to all electric grills by my name. Similar to the way someone might say, "I need a Kleenex," when asking for a facial tissue, or "May I please have a Q-tip?" when asking for a cotton swab on a stick, we have created a George Foreman brand. The George Foreman grill has become such a part of American culture that you can find it most anywhere—at wedding receptions, under Christmas trees, in college students' apartments, and in country music stars' million-dollar motor coaches. A magazine reporter told his sixteen-year-old son, who was much too young to remember my boxing career, that he was going to do an interview with George Foreman.

His son looked back at him quizzically. "Do you mean the grill guy?"

That's right, I'm the grill guy, and our products are known for their quality and value. Regardless, though, whether our product is the grill, an industrial strength cleaner, a new fast-food line, or a piece of hospital equipment, the "brand" has to spell excellence and trust. When people buy something or invest in something with my name on it, they know it is top notch. They buy with confidence because they have confidence in me. If they are investing in something that bears my name, they know it may be a risky venture at first, but it is not a pipe dream or a scam, and it will *never* be fraudulent. No matter what the product or business I am promoting, whether it is the George Foreman grill or a new health food chain, they are buying George Foreman, not simply the product. If it has my name on it, people know it is good.

In the same way, make your work known for its excellence. How do you establish a reputation of producing quality work? Simple: if it has your name on it, whether it is a report to your supervisor at work or a pizza that somebody is going to deliver, do your work with such a high degree of integrity and excellence that all people with whom you deal have the confidence that you are giving them the best possible service and best quality products.

People buy into the brand name before they buy the product, and for the Knockout Entrepreneur, the name and the person are often one and the same. That comes back to character and competence. If your name is on the product, you can be certain that people are judging your product by your personal character.

CHARACTER COUNTS

General Norman Schwarzkopf, who was catapulted to fame through his strong leadership during the Gulf War of 1991, put it this way: "People choose their leaders based on character. I judge character not by how men deal with their superiors, but by how they deal with their subordinates. That's how you find out what the character of a man truly is."

Your character influences everything you do, and it especially shows in the way you treat people you lead, supervise, or employ. Be generous with your praise of the people over whom you have authority, whether in the office, in the field, in the manufacturing area, or in your home. Let them know you appreciate them. I like to tell my children, "I believe in you. I trust you." Get those kinds of words into your vocabulary, and use them often. Tell your kids, "You are going to do great things. You can do so much more than I have done. And you will do it better!" When people receive that kind of encouragement from someone they consider a leader, they can do almost anything.

COMPETENCE MATTERS TOO

Along with character, you and your business must develop a consistent track record of competence—demonstrating your ability to get a job done, a product delivered on time or ahead of schedule, with no gaffes or defects. People will be attracted to a proven winner. Again and again, I've heard people say two priceless words about the George Foreman grill: "It works!" It works, and it works well because we are committed to excellence in our company. We are continually working to improve our products and our services, and we are never satisfied with "that's good enough."

I refuse to advertise or attempt to sell anything that conflicts with my values. If at all possible, I prefer to personally use anything I advertise, but I certainly won't advertise something I don't believe in or wouldn't use. One well-known actress became a laughingstock in 2007 when she was featured in Pizza Hut commercials and then she later admitted that she didn't eat pizza and she didn't even like tomatoes or most of the other ingredients in pizza. If your name is associated with the product, it better be good and you better like it!

I have my name on all sorts of products, everything from various George Foreman food products to George Foreman's Knock-Out Pro Green cleaning products for kitchens, carpets, and power washers to music albums, books, and even the George Foreman iGrill, a computer storage device for keeping all sorts of cooking data together. You hook it up to a computer with Internet access and you can download a recipe, including the type of food, how much you are cooking, and the cooking temperature you will need to make it just right. If you are running late, you can send a message through your computer and have the iGrill get dinner started for you while you are on the way home. The iGrill even glows and increases in brightness when it is time to take the food out.

I've also had vitamins, cookbooks, and other health and fitness items with my name on them. My clothing line, the George Foreman Signature Collection, is sold exclusively through the Casual Male Big & Tall retail stores. Regardless of the product, customers are buying George Foreman and my wholesome, hearty image, so it becomes even more important that I keep that image clean.

NEVER COMPROMISE YOUR INTEGRITY

When it comes to ethics, always take the high road; don't compromise a bit. Sure, rabbit punches (illegal punches behind the head) sometimes happen; sometimes people hit below the belt, but that doesn't mean you have to do it. Funny thing about those kinds of punches: the person who throws the second illegal punch is the one who gets caught. Whether it is in boxing, professional football, or business, sometimes tempers flare and someone will take a cheap shot at you. But if you allow yourself to respond in kind, you are most likely going to be the one penalized. Keep your business dealings aboveboard, and if somebody does you dirty, just shake off the dust and keep going. Don't lower your values or your standards.

It's not always easy. In 2002, I was ready to launch wholeheartedly into a campaign to promote a line of meat products and other foods in conjunction with a company in Omaha. But then we discovered that the company was going to use my name to promote coffee and frozen meat products of which I did not approve. It was a mess, and it was embarrassing. Eventually the only way to deal with it was to allow the company to go bankrupt. Now I am much more careful about striking deals that will perpetuate only the image we have established for our brands.

My sons George Jr. and George III help me with the George Foreman brand, and we sort through dozens and dozens of endorsement offers every week. We don't accept many, not necessarily because they aren't good products, but one key to success is keeping your name out there in the public's mind, and keeping it associated with excellence, while not allowing your name to be spread too thin. So we are quite particular about which products will carry my name and picture. I try all potential products before even considering a deal, testing them on one of the toughest focus groups in the world—my wife and ten children. I have an ethics clause in my contract prohibiting the use of my name in promoting alcohol, tobacco, pornography, or gambling.

WORK HARD TO GET LUCKY

Some people say being a successful businessperson is all about luck—being at the right place at the right time. I don't believe that. I do believe the popular quote "The harder I work, the luckier I get." Oh sure, I was saved by the bell a few times in my boxing career. There were some rounds when I wasn't sure whether it was the bell in the ring or my head that was ringing, and had that round not ended just then, I might not have gotten the rest I needed to recuperate and come back to fight another round. But as a boxer, I couldn't rely on luck; I preferred to make my own luck. As a business-person, I try to do the same thing.

Don't wait for the lucky deal, for the interest rates to be just right, for the stock market to go up or down, or for circumstances to be perfect for your business. Sometimes luck happens, but don't count on it. Keep fighting, keep working hard, and keep competing with excellence until the last bell rings.

Two friends were playing tennis one day. They were about equal in their abilities, but one was a strong competitor, and the other was dogging it, merely doing enough to get by. Finally, the competitor stopped his friend in midserve and shouted, "Wait a minute! Look at you. You really don't want to win, do you?"

"Of course I do," his friend replied, letting his racket drop to his side.

"No, you don't. And I can tell it. You're not even trying. If you want to win, you have to act like you want to win."

Whether in sports or business, the same principle is true. You won't become successful or significant by moping around the office or dogging it out there in the field. If you want to be successful, you must show the world—and most important, show yourself—that you intend to be success-ful. Align your behavior with your goals, doing things that are good for others, not merely things that are good for you. Your clients will soon catch on, and they will know that if the product has your name on it, they can count on it. You'll know that your branding is a success when there are two products readily available in the same location, and the customer chooses yours because it has your name on it. According to the book of Proverbs, a good name is rather to be chosen than fine gold. That's true in every area of life, but especially so in business.

A reporter in England once interviewed me about my success as an entrepreneur. Talking about the grill, he rubbed his chin as he spoke, "I say, old chap, what a brilliant name for a gadget—the Lean, Mean, Fat-Reducing Grilling Machine."

"No," I told him with a smile, "the genius was in calling it the *George Foreman* Lean, Mean, Fat-Reducing Grilling Machine."

If a product, service, or project has your name on it, make it good. Do it right the first time. It is your reputation, your character on the line, so don't compromise on quality or anything that might impugn your integrity. Knockout Entrepreneurs know the value of a good name.

KNOCKOUT IDEAS
TO STIMULATE YOUR SUCCESS

1. Life is not what you find, but what you create out of what you discover about yourself. What are some of the raw materials you have been given from which you can carve a successful life?

2. No matter what career path you choose, you must commit yourself to working hard if you hope to succeed. More than any other factor, success is most often attributable to hard work. List several areas where you have been complacent, lazy, or inattentive. What can you do to work harder in these areas? If you say, "Nothing," start the process over. Remember, being mediocre is easy, but attaining success takes work.

3. In many areas of life, there is often a fine line between winning and losing, between doing your best and doing something less. Whatever

you do, make your product or service the best. Think of a recent product, project, or service you provided. On a scale of one to ten, how well did you meet expectations? Consider two or three ways in which you can raise that number.

CHAPTER FIVE

PAIN IS THE MIDDLE NAME OF THE GAME

B oxing can be a wonderfully invigorating sport, and professional boxing can be quite lucrative, but it can also be an extremely painful way
to make a living. For one thing, getting hit goes with the territory. It
is to be expected. As a boxer, you know you are going to take some shots. You
don't cover up and cry every time you get hit; you know some hard blows are
coming, and you prepare for them. You know pain will come sooner or later if
you stay in the ring long enough. Pain is the middle name of the game.

Yet only if you are in the fight do you have a chance to win. Nevertheless,
you must understand that bruises, cuts, body aches, broken bones, swollen
eyes, and a puffy face are to be expected. Worse yet, sometimes you may
experience illegal head butts, rabbit punches, and of course, the dreaded
knockdown.

All of this goes with the territory. The only way to avoid these mishaps is to never enter the fracas or to quit. In fact, if you have not experienced any of the aforementioned setbacks, you should probably evaluate what you are doing with your time because you haven't really entered the fight.

The same could be said of striving for success in any field. In every endeavor of value, it is inevitable that you will encounter painful experiences. Life is full of hard knocks, and the more successful, influential, and significant you become, the harder the knocks that will come your way. You can be certain that if you are in the game, you are going to get bumps and bruises. You are going to take some shots and suffer setbacks, some of which will be downright embarrassing. That doesn't mean you should throw in the towel; it means you are making progress in the game. Don't be overly discouraged when troubles come or when your best-laid plans collapse right before your eyes. Instead, just keep fighting; keep pushing yourself back into the ring, and sooner or later you will prevail.

The people observing you during your fight are watching closely to see how you handle setbacks. That's why it is important that those around you—especially those who have an interest in your success or defeat—see nothing breaking your will or daunting your resolve to continue the fight.

Your opponents will be watching like hawks to detect any area of weakness in you—in your words, body language, or countenance. If they see an opportunity to attack, they will inevitably attempt to exploit your weaknesses. Make sure they see only your renewed sense of purpose and a determination to win.

DON'T LET DISAPPOINTMENTS KEEP YOU DOWN

Failures and disappointments may come; you may feel down, but never allow yourself to stay down. Don't give up; get up and move on. The Good

Book says that weeping may last for a night, but joy comes in the morning. Push away the weeping so you can be productive again.

I've had some business setbacks in my career. In addition to the microfilm company that went bust, I had the venture known as George Foreman Beef, in which we entered partnerships with meatpacking houses. It seemed like a natural companion product for the Lean, Mean, Fat-Reducing Grilling Machine, but for some reason, the George Foreman meat products never caught on with the public.

The company was comprised of a bunch of good friends, and that may have been our fatal flaw. With a group like that, nobody was willing to say that something wasn't a good idea.

Was I disappointed? Of course. I wanted the business to succeed. My name was on those meat products and they didn't sell. But I was determined. If that idea didn't work, I'd put together some other ideas and get them out there. Sooner or later, something would be a hit.

Some people don't have to deal with business or career setbacks so much as they have to work through physical disabilities, accidents, illnesses, or tragedies. For most of my life, I've been rather healthy, so I am happy to say that I've not had to deal with diseases. But I do recall a time early in my boxing comeback when I suffered a severe physical setback that had dire implications for my dreams, desires, and hopes for my career.

In 1987, I had made up my mind to get back into boxing, but in the ten years since I had been in training, I had allowed my weight to balloon up to 315 pounds. I planned my physical workout routine to firm up my muscles as I lost the weight, and part of my regimen involved chopping down trees with a hatchet. I had done something similar while training for previous fights, using an axe to chop trees for fifteen or twenty minutes at a time. Before beginning, I took my axe to a friend who had a machine shop, and he sharpened the blade to a razor sharp edge. The axe exercises proved extremely effective in helping me drop the excess weight and firm up my torso.

About two months before my first fight, I was outside chopping on an oak tree, when suddenly the axe head ricocheted off the tree and slammed into my leg, slicing through the flesh all the way down to the bone. Instantly, blood gushed down my leg into my boot. I was in a mental zone, a focused training mode, so although the pain seared through my leg, I was not about to let it keep me from training. I sat down on the ground, took off my boot and sock, and used the sock as a sort of tourniquet above the spot where the blade had gashed me. Then I picked up the axe and began whaling away at the tree again.

My son George Jr. was with me and expressed his concern. "Ahh, Dad, don't you think you should be a little more cautious?" he offered.

I smiled at him and said, "Son, if I'd have been cautious, you wouldn't be here." I continued chopping on the tree until I finished my workout. As George Jr. drove me back to the house, I kept telling myself the whole time, *I'm in training for a fight. This can't be anything serious!*

Once I got a good look at the wound, however, I knew I had never had an injury quite like this. "I have to go to the doctor," I told Joan.

"Okay, let me drive," Joan said.

"Naah. I'm fine. I can drive," I said, hobbling toward the car. I kept telling myself, *Sure, I can drive because this cut can't be anything*. It's a wonder we made it to the doctor's office because the pain had really begun to set in as I drove. Every move of my foot on the car's pedals caused me to wince.

Sure enough, when the doc took a look, he told me that the deep cut had gone all the way to the bone. He used a large number of sutures to sew me back together.

After he finished, I said to him, "Doc, I gotta get back to runnin' and choppin' again. I have an important boxing match coming up in about two months."

"Well, I don't think you're going to be doing much running for a while," he said.

"Oh, this is nothing." I nodded toward my bandaged leg.

"Mmm, I don't think you'll be able . . ."

"Yeah, right," I said. "I gotta be able to run."

The next day I headed out of the house to run, but I could barely walk. I had to hop on one leg just to move around the house.

My mental state bounced back and forth between being mad and disappointed. I had scheduled a boxing match and had been training for several months, and now with only weeks before the fight, I couldn't run. What was I to do?

I decided that I would continue my training as best I could. I got a stool and placed it in front of the punching bag, and then I had my brother Robert hold the bag firmly while I sat on the stool and punched the bag from a sitting position. I couldn't do anything else. The pain was intense, but I didn't dare take anything for it because the drug might remain in my system. In boxing, as in most sports, almost any unusual substance—even over-the-counter painkillers—found in a drug test would be enough to eliminate a boxer from the competition. I just gritted my teeth and kept punching. Day after day I sat on that stool and punched that bag. In the process I developed a different punching style, using my upper body movement more than my lower body and legs. Eventually, when I finally was able to get back on my feet, I was ready for the boxing match.

That injury could have wiped out my comeback career before it even started. But I was determined to work my way back to the top of the boxing world. The kids at my youth center were depending on me, and I wasn't about to let them down.

STAY IN LINE—PATIENCE PAYS

In boxing, the minimum amount of time a fighter might train for a bout is two to three months, and some boxers may allow much more time to prepare for a match. That's why it always surprises me when I meet people who are discouraged or impatient because their start-up business is not flourishing after a few weeks, or their careers are not moving ahead as rapidly as they might like. We are so accustomed to instant gratification that we forget the old axiom "Good things come to those who wait."

I tell my kids to get in line and keep fighting to get ahead, but to understand that they may have to advance slowly. Keep fighting anyway. Some people will drop out as the fight intensifies; others will get out when they realize that you are going to be there, that you aren't giving up or going away.

If you are standing in line, waiting to apply for a job, to get into college, to earn a scholarship, or to pursue a new opportunity, be persistent but also be patient. There may be a hundred people in that line right now, but many of them will grow discouraged or offended, and some won't want to do what is required. If you remain steadfast, you will move ahead merely by attrition, without having to do a thing—except stay in line. The same is true with a start-up business. There may be ten or twenty other stores or shops like yours, but if you provide a quality product or service in a clean, friendly environment, you will draw your share of the business by staying where you are. Sure, you should always seek to be innovative, but patience is a virtue that many people have lost when it comes to career building. They see someone who is successful, and they assume that it took a short time to get there.

Consider the long road back to the top that I had to travel. At one time I was the world heavyweight champion, and many professional boxing buffs called me the greatest puncher of all time. But when I started on my comeback, it took me more than three and a half years to earn back another shot at the title I had once owned. Not three and a half months—three and a half *years*! But before I started, I made up my heart and mind that I was willing to work hard, be patient, stay in line, and keep making progress toward my goal. I knew that if I did those things, one day I'd be the world heavyweight champion again, even if I was in my midforties when it happened.

At first it was almost embarrassing to be offered some of the boxing matches with less talented fighters, but I took them anyhow. I fought my way through them and stayed in line.

One friend told me, "I'm not going to take a match for only three thousand dollars."

"Three thousand dollars?" I said. "I'll take it." And I did. Before long, I was fighting for $5,000, then $10,000, $25,000, and then a hundred times that much and more. Why? Because I was the best? Probably not. Mostly, I kept earning the right to move ahead because I stayed in line, did a good job where I was, and attempted to capitalize on whatever opportunity presented itself.

PRAYER—TAP INTO POWER

Be patient and persistent; perhaps most important, be prayerful. If you truly want to be successful, you must pray. I had raw talent, but I can tell you for certain that I could not have done what I did in my career had it not been for the power of prayer. I could not have succeeded without the help of God, and neither can you.

Every once in a while, I'd get tired of standing in line, or I'd get a little down. Right at that point, I'd receive a bit of encouragement from God. Sometimes it came in the form of a dream or a fresh insight; sometimes the encouragement came through a sermon or a song. That's all I needed to keep going. "God, are You looking at me? Are You paying attention to what I'm doing? Oh! You are! Well, thank You! I'll keep working harder."

If you will pray, God will answer, and in His own way He will let you know that He is with you as you stay in line. When you pray, don't ask God for stuff; ask Him for solutions. He might give you a fresh idea about how to solve a problem or a vision for a new venture in your career or business; He might guide you to step out in faith and attempt to meet someone who can help you along the road to success. Best of all, sometimes He simply lets you know that He is with you.

At one point in my life, I was having a tough time and traveling a hard road, so I went home to Houston to my aunt's house. While I was resting there, I fell fast asleep and experienced a rather unusual dream. In my dream I saw and heard a country singer performing a song:

Once in a while, Lord tells me that He loves me.
Once in a while, Lord tells me that He cares.

I had never heard the song before; nor had I ever seen the performer. Yet it was almost as though God put the message on a billboard, and through that dream He reassured me, "I love you, George." That's all I needed to know. That bit of encouragement got me through the next three years.

"My grace is sufficient for you, for My strength is made perfect in weakness." Those words were first given to the apostle Paul when he was praying to be healed of some sort of thorn in his flesh. God did not heal Paul during his lifetime, which tells me that there won't always be an easy way out. But God's answer to Paul's prayer motivated him to stay in the line. "Most gladly I will rather boast in my infirmities!" he said. Paul received a bit of encouragement, and that's all it took to keep him going. I felt the same way as I prayed. I knew that God was with me.

In every career, a lot of time must be spent standing in line. Almost all true success requires perseverance and patience. You may be tempted to think you are wasting your time, but if you will simply trust, work hard, and be faithful, God will be there with you. Especially when you are praying, "God, please help me," rather than saying, "I'm going to make it on my own!"

Even Knockout Entrepreneurs sometimes get hurt or discouraged. Sure, you may experience pain and difficulties, but every situation, no matter how rough or painful, can be an opportunity to learn and grow. If you will hang in there and keep doing the right thing long enough, your success will come. Just don't drop out of the line. As a Knockout Entrepreneur, you can get up and face each day saying, "My time is coming. It might be today, or it might be tomorrow, but I know that sooner or later, it will be my time to shine."

KNOCKOUT IDEAS
TO STIMULATE YOUR SUCCESS

1. Most of us—even boxers—try to avoid any more pain than necessary, but it usually catches up to all of us sooner or later. How are you stronger today because of the pain you have encountered in your life?

2. Nobody likes to remain on hold for long, especially when it comes to a career or a relationship. Yet that waiting process is not wasted time. Stay in line and keep working hard. Your efforts will not go unnoticed.

CHAPTER SIX

DO THE UNEXPECTED—THE COUNTERINTUITIVE ENTREPRENEUR

Fake, feign, punch—when others expect you to go one way, you can often fool them by doing the unexpected. It works in boxing, and it often works in business and other areas of life too.

For instance, often I recognize that I could do an effective endorsement or provide some other service for certain clients, products, or companies. It isn't their job to find me; I'm on the lookout for them. I am constantly looking for ways to humble myself and show them that I can do a good job for them. They may be afraid to approach me about working together, or they may be reluctant for some other reason, so I do all I can to show that I am approachable. Of course, this flies in the face of the modern success theories that say in order to be successful you must toot your own horn and remind people how great you are. So much of pop psychology says to watch out for number one because if you don't take care of you, nobody else will. Businessmen have told me, "George, don't be so easygoing. Don't let people take advantage of you. This is business. You have to be hard and demanding; you have to be aggressive."

That may work for some people, but I've discovered that the most aggressive thing I can do is to be humble. The Bible says that the meek shall inherit the earth, and I believe that. Meekness is not weakness. Meekness is often described as "power under control." You can be strong and powerful, and yet remain under control and humble.

Some people are afraid to express humility because they think that it will erode the respect of their peers or their employees. So they tout the fact that "this is *my* company, and we'll do things *my* way." There are many businesses run by executives who are obsessed with guarding their company, their esteem, and their prestige; meanwhile their profits are disappearing. And if they look closely, they often discover that their best employees are disappearing too. Why? Because a paycheck isn't enough to keep Knockout Entrepreneurs inspired. They have to feel that they are significant, that what they are doing matters, that they are contributing something good.

Popular radio and television show host Dave Ramsey is the author of the best-selling book *The Total Money Makeover*, and he is an on-air financial advisor to millions of people every day. In his live seminars, Dave tells of an experiment done by some psychology students at the University of California, Berkeley, in which they hired a group of workers to dig a ditch and offered to pay them a fair but average wage. About halfway through the day, the workers were instructed to fill in the ditch—the same ditch they had just spent half the day digging. "Why are we doing this?" one of the workers asked.

"Oh, it's just an experiment," came the reply.

"Do you mean that we are not digging this ditch to put something in it? To lay a water line or gas line, some telephone cables or something?"

"No, it is just a ditch, and you did a great job," the boss said. "You can get your day's pay, and we'll be right back here tomorrow morning. And tomorrow we are going to pay you double what you made today."

The following morning 40 percent of the workers didn't show up at the job site. But those who came back to work received twice the pay as the day before, simply to dig the same ditch. About midway through the day, once again the project boss came by and said, "Okay, guys, now let's fill in that ditch again."

The men grumbled and a few made other nasty comments, but they filled in the ditch. That evening the project boss said, "I just want you to know that tomorrow we're going to dig this ditch again, and we're going to double your pay again!"

But the next morning 40 percent of the remaining workers failed to show up for work. Why? Because money wasn't enough to keep them motivated. They needed to feel that their work mattered, that their lives were involved in something significant. They wanted their work to provide meaning, a sense of purpose, a feeling of accomplishment—and perhaps most of all, *significance*.[1]

Sadly, so many executives give the impression that the business is all about them, their wealth, their prosperity. They get so caught up in themselves that they miss the fact that the people who help make them great are leaving to find employment in other places, where the work has meaning— where the boss is willing to humble him- or herself to the point of serving the employees rather than using them for personal gain.

CAN HUMILITY REALLY BE LEARNED?

Serving your clientele and your employees well does not require you to be proud and arrogant, to puff yourself up and tell everyone how great you are.

No, one of the most counterintuitive secrets of success is to develop the trait of humility.

"Now, wait a minute, George," I can almost hear you saying. "How can you develop humility? Either you're humble or you're not."

That's where a lot of people miss the key to success and significance. Sure, some people are naturally humble—but not too many. Why? Because we are all born selfish, and we tend to feed our selfishness throughout our lives. If you are going to buck against selfishness, it will happen only because you are *willing* to be humble.

But you need to understand something about true humility. Being humble does not mean that you think of yourself as beneath other people or, worse yet, that you regard yourself as a worthless piece of humanity. Far from it! If you don't have anything going for yourself and you are a do-nothing person, don't confuse that with humility. Most likely, that's just laziness. As someone said, "People with humility don't think less of themselves. They just think of themselves less."[2] Truly humble people usually have a lot going for themselves; they are genuinely successful; they are really impressive and could rightfully toot their own horns, but most don't. Why? Because they have realized that their success cannot be laid at their own feet. Other people have helped them along the way. Usually a *lot* of other people have had some part in shaping the life of the truly successful person.

No doubt you have benefited by the efforts or contributions of many helpful and generous people in your life—maybe financially generous, but more important, generous with the most precious commodity of all, their time: their willingness to share their dreams and ideas with you and to mentor you over breakfast or help guide you toward the right career choices. If you look carefully, you will discover that everything good about your life to date is a collaboration between you and a lot of other people.

When you know that your success is not all because of your efforts, it is much easier to be humble. You don't need to throw your weight around or try to impress everybody with how talented, wealthy, or important you are. Nor do you need to intimidate people to get what you want. A truly humble person does not abuse his power or position. Most truly successful individuals I've met have an almost childlike awe of their success; they can hardly believe it! They see their significance in using their material wealth or personal accomplishments to help other people succeed, and they are almost always extremely grateful.

I like to take time almost every day just to say thank You to the good Lord for the people who have contributed to helping me become the person I am today. Not all of those people were positive influences; through some of them, I discovered what I *didn't* want to be in life. But others helped me in ways that I can never repay, except by doing my best to help someone else. When you take a few moments to acknowledge the people who have assisted you in your life, suddenly humility is a natural by-product of gratitude. Thanking God for His help and for the help of so many others in my life reminds me each day that I owe all that I am to Him and to the people He has allowed to enter my life. That alone is often enough to develop a sense of modesty and humility in a person. You find yourself wanting to toot somebody else's horn—especially God's—rather than your own.

Maybe that's why most genuinely humble men and women listen more than they talk. They are sincerely interested in the opinions of others, and they always take a variety of viewpoints into consideration before making a decision.

For the humble person, success is never simply about herself; it is always about others too. That's why she treats other people with dignity and respect, whether that other person delivers the newspaper each morning, waits on the table at the restaurant, or serves as the president of a major company. If you want to be successful, you must realize that there are no inferior people or superior people. All are worthy of respect and fair treatment.

I've noticed, too, that most truly successful people love to laugh. We sure enjoy laughter in the Foreman family! You probably enjoy a good laugh too. But be careful. You can tell a lot about a person by *what* he laughs at. Does he laugh at crude or obscene humor? Does she laugh at someone else's mistakes or failures? Do we laugh at other people's appearances, disabilities, quirks, or idiosyncrasies over which they have no control? A humble person loves to laugh, but his sense of humor and his jokes are usually at his own expense, not at the expense of others.

Now here's the marvelous truth about humility. You might think that if you are humble, people are going to disrespect you, take advantage of you, or treat you like a doormat. Nope. Not unless you encourage them to treat you like that. Most people will respect you more; you'll win a lot of new friends, and your old friends will be amazed! People will want you on their teams; they will want to do business with you because they realize that you are just as concerned about their success as you are your own.

You will not succeed by putting other people down or climbing over other people—kicking, scratching, and clawing your way to the top. No, just the opposite; you will succeed as you humble yourself and seek to build up other people, focusing not merely on your own success but on theirs as well.

COUNTERINTUITIVE COURAGE

Sometimes you need to have humility to do something different, and sometimes to be a counterintuitive person, doing something unexpected, you need courage. For instance, after the George Foreman grill was tremendously successful, the good folks from Salton, a large houseware appliance manufacturing company, came to me with an offer to buy the licensing rights to George Foreman electrical appliances. I had seen the grill grow from nothing, and it was not easy to let go of it. It was my baby. Not only that, it was a profit-making machine, so much so that I sometimes worried that people thought we might be printing money in my garage! The grill just kept making money for my family and me. Why would anyone want to rock that boat?

But the more I considered the offer, the more it made sense to me. I was in the business of selling. I began to ask myself, *If someone wanted to buy ten pieces of product, would I sell them? Sure I would. Well, what if they wanted to buy twenty? Yep, I'd sell. And if they wanted to buy all of the product?*

I decided to sell the rights. We worked out a mutually satisfactory deal in which I could still be involved in all the marketing campaigns as the main spokesperson. We built in written guarantees that the George Foreman grill could not be used to promote products I did not support. The brand can never be used to promote alcoholic beverages, for example. I still received royalties from the grill and could participate in development of new products. It was a win-win situation.

Could I have hung on to the license? Sure, but sometimes you just have to let go and move on. You can't be scared; you have to take a risk. Sometimes you give now and you will gain later. You can't be afraid to step out in faith; you have to take a chance sometimes, even if everyone else thinks you've lost your mind for doing so. But all of life involves risk. When you start a business, you are taking a risk; when you get on an airplane, you are taking a risk. We take dozens of risks every day. The most nerve-racking risks, however, may not be some extreme dare or challenge, but taking a risk on another human being.

GIVE SOMEONE A CHANCE

Probably one of the best-known boxing promoters in history is a man named Don King. Famous more for his outlandish, bombastic outbursts and behavior, as well as his erratically spiked hair, Don was relatively unknown when he came to me, asking to promote one of my fights. I was heavyweight champion of the world at the time, making a substantial amount of money. I didn't really need to take a risk on a relatively unknown fight promoter, much less one with Don's dubious reputation.

"Give me an opportunity to promote one of your fights, George," he asked humbly.

"Well, I don't know, Don," I replied, having a hard time keeping my eyes from drifting from his face up to his ridiculously styled hair. "You look like kind of a bad character to me."

"Oh, George. Everybody says I look bad. They just don't know me." Don launched into an extended emotion-packed explanation of why people didn't trust him. "But give me a chance, George. I can get you more money than anyone else has ever dreamed of." For a minute I almost thought Don was going to start crying as he dabbed at his eyes.

I looked him over again. He was quite a character, but I liked characters. For all his strange appearance and mannerisms, something about Don told me that he might just be able to pull off this fight. I looked him right in the eyes and said, "Okay, Don. I'm going to give you a chance. I'm going to sign a contract right here, right now. Take it to my attorney and tell him to work out the details. You put together a letter of credit for five million dollars for me, but there's only one stipulation."

"Anything, George. You name it."

"You gotta deliver Muhammad Ali," I said.

"I'll do it, George," King said brashly. But then he stopped short. "But I'll have to give him five million too."

"That's fine," I said. I didn't care how much Ali got paid; I just wanted a chance to fight him. Besides, five million dollars was an enormous amount of money to me.

Don King negotiated the boxing match, and true to his word, he got Ali and he arranged a purse of five million dollars for each of us. I risked getting involved with Don, and he delivered. Unfortunately I lost the boxing match that later became known as the great Rope a Dope fight, and I guess I was the dope. Don, however, parlayed his newfound fame as a result of that fight to become one of the most successful boxing promoters of all time.

START AT THE BOTTOM, NOT THE TOP

When I made my return to boxing in the 1980s, rather than attempt to start out at the top, as so many other great boxers had tried to do and failed, I decided that I would start at the bottom. That didn't make sense to a lot of boxing observers. Why would a former heavyweight champion of the world be willing to start at the bottom, fighting men most people had never even heard of before they were booked to fight me? There was a method to my madness.

I had researched all those fighters who had come out of retirement because I wanted to discover why they hadn't succeeded. They were all great boxers, but they failed to ascend to the top again after they retired. Several had returned to the ring only to be drubbed back into retirement after suffering ignominious defeats. I concluded that they had taken the wrong approach.

When former heavyweight champ Joe Louis tried to make his comeback from retirement, he was immediately offered a shot at the title. Rocky Marciano almost killed Joe in that fight. Louis tried to get back to the top too quickly and wasn't ready. Former heavyweight champion Joe Frazier also came out of retirement to fight again. He trained for about a week and looked horrible in a losing effort.

The boxers coming out of retirement to fight again had one thing in common—they were on top when they left and thought they could start over at the top. That was their mistake; they tried to return to the top too quickly. They assumed they didn't have enough time to start over at the bottom.

My boxing advisors told me, "You'd better hurry up because time is running out for you." They wanted me to follow the same failed strategy as my retired predecessors: start over at the top while I still had some ability left. But I wasn't going to follow the others into failure. Instead, I decided to do the opposite.

Everyone thought I was crazy when I explained my plan. "I'm not going to try to get a title shot for several years. I'll start over at the bottom and slowly work my way back to the top."

My friends looked at me as though I had lost my mind, but I knew it would take at least three years to get my timing back. There was no other way around it.

Most great achievements have simple beginnings, so when you are trying something new or different, don't set your sights on the top job; just set your sights on the next job up from where you are. Whatever you hope to achieve, it all begins with a first step. Ask yourself, *How much do I really want this? Am I willing to put in the hard work and discipline that it will take to achieve this goal? Will I resolve to do whatever it takes to get where I want to go?* Remind yourself, *It is possible, and it is time to get started.*

DREAM BIG AND *DO* SOMETHING

Knockout Entrepreneurs are not just visionaries or dreamers; they are doers. They work hard at developing and providing products that serve people well. They don't dream of a new wave; they anticipate the wave's direction, see it coming, and find a way to ride it out in front of everyone else, creating an opportunity to succeed by providing something that other people truly want or need.

In my case I spent hundreds of hours watching boxing film and reading articles, trying to learn how I could improve my timing. I studied all the great boxers and researched old sports clippings. I read everything I could find about track, boxing, and even football in the 1930s through the 1950s. Perhaps they used techniques we'd forgotten about. My extensive research helped me become a smarter boxer than I was previously.

When I first started on the comeback trail, promoters and reporters often asked about my age. "How old are you really?" they'd ask.

At first, I tried to keep them guessing about my age. "I'm closer to fifty than I am to thirty," I'd tell them. But after a while, I realized that my age could be a plus. I turned it around and made my being older into a positive rather than a negative. In almost every interview, the question of my age came up. I didn't mind. In fact, I had a lot of fun with the subject during inter-views. "Mike Tyson says he's going to attack. Not me; I'm gonna hide!" I facetiously told reporters.

Rather than see myself as getting older, I chose to regard myself as graduating to a higher level in life. I've gained insights from every year I've lived. My experiences have added depth to my life, which has taught me to make better transitions as I've grown older. Instead of relying on abilities that become weaker over time, I've capitalized on skills that become stronger with age. You can do so too. Rather than focusing on what you can no longer do, place your emphasis on the things that you have learned by experience and can put into practice.

Many people fail not so much because of their mistakes; they fail because they are afraid to try. They fear being rejected, getting knocked down, or being embarrassed. Successful people, however, realize that rejection means that you move on to the next opportunity. Getting knocked down goes with the territory; failure is part of the learning process. Older entrepreneurs have a much higher success rate than younger entrepreneurs, often because they have learned from their mistakes. They know that the worst thing they can do is to do nothing.

TAKE THE FIRST STEP

Sometimes even when the odds are against you—when you don't have a contract, when people have rejected you or can't catch your vision—the best thing you can do is move on. If you must, start something on your own.

Chuck Wepner was a relatively unknown boxer in 1975, but he had earned a shot at the very well-known Muhammad Ali. Nobody expected Wepner to win, but on March 24, 1975, he went fifteen rounds with the heavyweight champion of the world. At one point in the ninth round, Wepner walloped Ali with a powerful right-hand punch to the champ's chin, sending Muhammad tumbling to the mat. Everyone in the arena—maybe even Wepner—was shocked! Ali got up, though, and went on to win the fight.

Most of the boxing world probably wrote Wepner off after his defeat, but a struggling actor who had watched the fight on television was inspired by Wepner's near miss. He had considered writing a screenplay about a boxer getting a once-in-a-lifetime title shot, but the actor didn't really think anyone would take the story seriously—until he saw Chuck Wepner deck Ali. It could happen.

The actor—who had never written a screenplay that anyone wanted to produce—went to work, writing furiously, pounding out a story line that he'd been thinking about for years. In less than a week, Sylvester Stallone had written the original screenplay for a movie he called *Rocky*. Even then, nobody seemed interested in producing the movie, so Stallone raised the money and produced and starred in his own movie. That movie won three Academy Awards and launched the subsequent *Rocky* movies as well as Stallone's legendary movie career. But it all started when Stallone stopped merely thinking about writing a screenplay and actually did it!

If you want to get ahead, if you want to succeed in life or be more successful than you are currently, you must get up and do something! And the sooner you start, the better your chances of being successful.

There's an old adage that says, "It is much easier to steer a moving boat rather than one that is tied up at the dock." If you want to get anywhere, you're going to have to push away from the dock.

What if you go in the wrong direction? No problem. Just realign your course in the right direction. But you'll never get anywhere just sitting there at the dock, waiting for something big to happen in your life. Push away from the dock, hoist your sails, crank up your motor, and watch a new world open right before your eyes.

DARE TO DO SOMETHING DIFFERENT

My greatest asset as a young boxer was my speed. The gifted boxer Sugar Ray Robinson told me, "It doesn't matter how you throw your punches as long as you can do it quickly." But after being retired from boxing for ten years, my speed and instincts had deteriorated.

As I studied the boxers who had tried to come back from retirement, I noticed they relied on the same techniques they used when they were younger. But they couldn't function at their previous performance level, and their opponents quickly sent them back into retirement.

Instead of following in their footsteps, I decided to try something different. If I hoped to win the championship again, I would have to find a way to compensate for my lack of speed. My immobility forced me to learn a new and different way to box. Even though I had the desire inside me to win the title, my physical skills didn't measure up to what they were when I was younger. My new style of boxing had to be completely different from the way I had moved around in the ring before. I also had to find another method for defending myself, such as changing the position of my hands for better protection.

Even in training, I had to make adjustments. I couldn't run fast anymore, but I could walk. Walking strengthened the muscles I needed for endurance. No longer would I depend on the quick knockout, but I decided to work on improving my stamina so I could stay in the ring for the full twelve rounds. That may sound like an easy task, but I had to spar with the young guys in the gym, and making all those adjustments wasn't easy at first.

After doing some soul-searching, I knew that I couldn't recapture the heavyweight title unless I first won the fight inside my mind. I had to believe I could win it before I could actually do it. So instead of being frustrated about learning a new way to box, I decided to prove to the world that no one is too old to start over.

With a renewed outlook, I realized my age could work to my advantage rather than as a disadvantage. All of my past experience gave me an edge over the younger boxers. When I first started boxing as a young man, I didn't know how to do anything. I didn't even know how to train for a fight. I couldn't skip rope. I couldn't hit the speed bags. Everything that I needed to learn seemed impossible then. Yet by the time I was twenty-four years old, I was considered the best at skipping rope, hitting the speed bags, and running in preparation for a boxing match.

Learning a new way to box wouldn't be as difficult as beginning from scratch. If I could start from the bottom and win the championship, surely

I could take my abilities to another level with a new technique and a better way to utilize my more mature skill set. The way I look at it, if you've already done something once, you can do it again. If you've started at the bottom and learned a particular skill, your experience puts you ahead of the game.

When I started on the comeback trail in the 1980s, many of my insider boxing friends said, "Go to Don King. After all you did for him, he owes you. Ask him to set up some fights for you. Don can help you because he is now involved in all the title matches."

"Now, wait a minute," I'd say. "Didn't I tell you that I helped make Don King?"

"Yes, George, you did. And we know that is true. Before you gave him a chance, he was just another wild-eyed fight promoter. Now he is one of the richest and most influential figures in boxing. When he needed you, you were there for him, George. Now you need Don King."

"Well, if I really made Don King," I mused, "I don't need him to remake me. If I hadn't had such a big influence on Don's success, then I may need him now. But if I gave Don King an opportunity to succeed, why can't I do the same thing for myself?"

"Yeah, but that's too much work," one of my friends protested.

"Well, that's what a human being is supposed to do," I replied. "We're not meant to sit around expecting someone else to take care of us. We're supposed to get out there and make our own opportunities."

I knew boxing better than Don King did. I gave him an opportunity to get big quickly, and Don took it and did well with it, but he never really knew what it was like to work his way up from the bottom. I did, and I felt certain in my heart and mind that I could do it again—if I wanted it badly enough to work harder than I'd ever worked before. My refusing to turn to Don for help wasn't about him and his willingness to repay a favor; it was about me and my willingness to work for what I wanted. Again, it was counterintuitive; it went against all boxing logic, but I knew it was the right way for me to proceed.

I put up posters to advertise my bouts, boxing in town after town, before small crowds and for very little money. I did grand openings at used car lots, signing autographs for anybody, fighting for a few hundred dollars, working my way up from the bottom. I became a joke to many boxing reporters. Talk show hosts teased, "George, you're fighting guys on a respirator."

"That's not true!" I replied, pretending to be insulted. "They have to be off the respirator for five days before I'll fight them!" But while everyone was laughing at me, I kept fighting my way up the boxing ranks, learning more with each match.

Finally, I was ready to sit down with Don King, who at that time was promoting Mike Tyson, the current heavyweight champion of the world. Don came to our meeting with a huge contract for a fight. "All right, George, just sign this," Don said as he spread out the papers, "and I'll get you the championship fight."

Don's flippancy almost insulted me. "Man, don't you understand?" I said. "I'm going to win this thing."

Don pulled out another contract from his briefcase. "Yep," he said, "and I have another contract for that!"

"Well, I'm going to be the champion of the world."

Don got upset. He stood up and said, "Not without me! Nobody—" Don stopped mid-thought, as though he suddenly realized to whom he was speaking. "I'm sorry, George," he quickly apologized. "I shouldn't have said that like that."

"It's okay, Don," I said. "But I am going to be the champion of the world again."

"Okay, George. Sure thing."

A week after I became the first man in history ever to come back from a retirement of ten years to win the heavyweight championship of the world for the second time, I called Don King. I think it nearly killed him, but Don graciously congratulated me.

It wasn't cockiness that made me feel that I could succeed on my own. I believed in God and in myself. If I had been relying on Don to remake my career, I might have been worried. I might have had cause to fear. But I knew where my strengths lay, and as long as I kept those priorities in order, I knew I would come out all right—and I did.

I felt the same way when it was time to turn loose of the George Foreman grill. If I really made the grill, then what did I have to fear? But if the grill made George Foreman, then I was in trouble. No machine is better than any human being. If I could take a grill and make it the best-selling electrical appliance in history, then I could do something similar with other products.

Of course, I was quick to give God the credit He so rightly deserves. Anyone who is truly a Knockout Entrepreneur knows where the success begins and to whom the praise and honor should return. When the grill became so phenomenally successful, I tried my best to always give God glory through it. "God did this for me," I would tell people. "God made this happen." If I really believe that—and I do—then I have nothing to fear about turning loose of my success.

Here's an important principle about being counterintuitive: In the ring you can't start out by faking and feigning an opponent and think that he's going to back off. He won't. He'll come after you with a vengeance and might possibly knock you right out of the ring!

Fakes and feigns are effective only if you come out swinging. Come out of the corner with your power shots blazing. Throw your first punches with as much effort as you possibly can. Hit the opponent with your best shots hard and early, and hit him often. Then when you fake or do something counterintuitive, your opponent will back away instinctively to keep from being hit hard again. But you have to take your best shot first; then you can put the competition to flight.

Promoters told me, "George, we're willing to pay you one hundred thousand dollars to fight this guy."

"No," I said. "I don't want to fight that guy yet. I'll fight this other guy."

"We're not going to pay you one hundred thousand dollars to fight that guy. He's not even an up-and-comer."

"Okay, fine," I'd say, and I would fight that same boxer in some small town for five thousand dollars. Some people thought I was undercutting my value, but it was a counterintuitive move. I knew that as soon as I won that fight for five thousand dollars, those same promoters would be back offering me twice as much. That's the way it happened too. The next time those promoters came around, they said, "Now, George, just who would you like to fight? We'll make that happen."

A key to taking counterintuitive steps is being ready to back up your words with actions. If you say to your boss, "I'm one of your best employees here. I'd like a raise, or I'm going to seek work elsewhere," you might be bluffing, hoping that your ultimatum will lead to a raise. You must be prepared for your boss to call your bluff and say, "Good-bye, and don't let the door hit you on your way out."

But if you raise your performance level to exceed expectations, and then go to your boss and say, "I've been our top performer for the past three months; I believe I deserve a raise," you are much more likely to get it. Always take your most powerful position first; then you can negotiate from a more secure stance.

FAITH—THE ULTIMATE COUNTERINTUITIVE

Here is another principle that has helped me in business as well as other aspects of life: *don't be afraid to step out on faith*. Let me explain. One of my favorite stories in the Bible is about a rambunctious fisherman named Peter, a fellow whom Jesus handpicked to be one of His disciples. One night Peter and his buddies were in a boat on the Sea of Galilee. Sometime between three o'clock in the morning and dawn, Jesus came walking toward them *on top of the water*! Peter and his friends were understandably frightened—wouldn't you be? They thought at first that Jesus was some sort of ghost. But Jesus called out to them and said, "Take courage, it is I; do not be afraid."

Peter must have been convinced, and he said, "Lord, if it is You, command me to come to You on the water."

And Jesus said, "Come on."

Now think about this. Peter was a professional fisherman. He knew how deep that lake was, and he knew the dangers of jumping out of the boat in the middle of the night. But he had so much faith that he stepped out of the boat—and started walking toward Jesus! He was doing fine too, having the time of his life, until the wind sprang up. When Peter saw the wind whipping up the waves, he got scared. His faith drooped, and his body dropped. He started to sink like a rock. He had to call out to Jesus to save him, so Jesus reached out His hand and caught Peter. Jesus asked him, "Oh, you of little faith, why did you doubt?"

If you are going to be a Knockout Entrepreneur, don't be afraid to take steps of faith. Who knows? You might just walk on water. It won't be the elements, lack of good business principles, or anything else that sinks your business or prevents you from being successful. It is your faith that keeps you up or lets you down. You must have faith if you are in business. Your faith will hold you up, even when the wind is blowing hard in your face.

When the storms rise all around you, you don't have to go under if you have faith; put your trust in the Lord, and keep walking.

After the George Foreman grill did so well, I was almost walking on air! The grill continued selling in incredibly large numbers, and there came a time when I wanted to take a new walk of faith, so I let go of the safe, secure boat and took a step into the deep water. My faith is real, so I knew that if we did it once with the grill, we could do it again with other products too.

You might be saying, "Come on, George. What does faith have to do with it? We're talking business here, not religion."

Maybe so, but we all know that "as a man thinks in his heart, so he is," and so he becomes. And even beyond that, consider this: one of the most counterintuitive things you can do is to have faith in God, not because all people in business are atheists, but because your faith shows people who work with you and do business with you that you are not only an independent Knockout Entrepreneur, but you are a person under authority as well. It says that you are accountable to Someone other than yourself.

LET PEOPLE KNOW THAT YOU ARE ACCOUNTABLE

Accountability flies in the face of many modern business practices. Most entrepreneurs would prefer being Lone Rangers. If you stop to think about it, though, letting people know that you are ready and willing to account for your actions raises the confidence level of people who may want to hire you or do business with you. Why? A danger of doing business with super-creative people or entrepreneurs is that they may not be in the same business tomorrow. They may be off chasing some other dream, working on a new invention. You may not have a board of directors or a supervisor who can look you in the eye and say, "I don't think that is a good idea" or "Maybe you should reconsider that business decision." As a Knockout Entrepreneur, you can usually do whatever you want to do with your business.

People you do business with will have more confidence when they know that you are not a capricious person, simply following the whims of your heart and mind. You will do much better in business when you can consistently show that your decisions and actions are not just spur-of-the-moment ideas, but well-thought-out choices, and that you are accountable to someone. But to whom are you accountable if you are the boss, the leader, the main decision maker, the voice of your product or service? You may be accountable to a good spouse and to your family and friends, but your business associates will trust you more when they know that you are accountable to a greater authority, Someone bigger than you.

No, I'm not talking about the Internal Revenue Service, although in the United States we are accountable to pay our taxes honestly and correctly. I'm talking about being accountable to God. When your customers or business associates know that you are going to be checking in with the good Lord, and more important, that He will be examining your "books," it does not make you smaller in their eyes. It makes you larger. It gives you more credibility and authority rather than less. That's why having faith is one of the most counterintuitive things you can do in business.

It always takes courage to go a different direction or to set your sail against the wind. You have to be willing to bend your own will—what you want—for the benefit of the company. The more people you have working with you or for you, the more counterintuitive you must be.

I heard a story about a senior executive who looked out the window of his corner office high atop the building with his name on the front. As he looked down into the parking lot below, he thought to himself, *I need to work harder. I have to make the car payments for every one of my employees parked in that lot.* That man is a success. He is not simply working for another dollar or a gold watch or a nice retirement. He is working to serve other people.

Theodore Roosevelt is often credited with saying, "In any moment of decision, the best thing you can do is the right thing. The next best thing you can do is the wrong thing. And the worst thing you can do is nothing." I agree! When you look at a problem that others say is impossible to solve, instead of sulking in the corner with them, jump right in the middle of the ring and look for a new angle, perhaps a bold decision that needs to be made. Often the bolder the decision, the more successful the outcome. As one insightful fellow put it, "It is better to err on the side of daring than the side of caution."[3]

ADMIT WHEN YOU ARE WRONG

A word of caution: when you know you have made the best decision you can with the knowledge available to you, own up to things that don't go well, and take responsibility. Simply put: admit when you are wrong. Many businessmen are reluctant to do that. It goes against their business logic, but the results speak for themselves. Your coworkers, employees, family members, and friends will respect you more when you admit your mistakes.

One of the more popular American television shows in recent years is the Emmy Award–winning program *My Name Is Earl*. The concept of the sitcom is that Earl, a petty crook who has had frequent run-ins with the law, loses his recently won $100,000 lottery ticket when he is hit by a car. While in the hospital, he decides to turn his life around. He makes a list of all the bad things he has ever done and decides he is going to make right all the things he has done wrong. The show is both funny and poignant, as Earl attempts to clean up his past messes.

We all wish we could go back and clean up some of the messes we have made. And some of us have made some pretty big messes!

For many years I refused to apologize to anybody, even if I knew that I had been wrong. But one of the first things I did after I met the good Lord was to sit down and start calling all the people in my life whom I had hurt. I don't mean in the ring; I'm talking about hurting them in life. I offended them somehow; I used some for my selfish gratification, and there were some to whom I was just downright mean!

Most of my apologies didn't have much to do with my past business, although I did call and ask forgiveness of a number of people who had formerly worked with me. I'd call and say something like, "I want to ask your forgiveness for hurting you. You didn't do anything mean to me. The past is over and done. Let's move on." Something as simple as that.

Some people didn't understand; they might have thought that I was trying to pull something on them, or maybe they had never heard someone genuinely ask forgiveness before, so they didn't know how to respond. That was okay. I wasn't doing it for them; I was doing it because I needed to do it for me. I needed to have a clean conscience. It took me more than two years to get in touch with all the people I had hurt—I had hurt a bunch. Even to this day I'm occasionally reminded of someone my life affected negatively, and I try to contact him or her and apologize.

As I said, most of those apologies had nothing to do with my business— or did they? Do you have any idea how good it feels to operate with a clean slate? Do you know what it is like to sit down in a room to negotiate a deal without fearing that anything from the past is going to pop up and spoil it for you? I do. And if there were no other reasons to learn how to apologize and admit your errors, that confidence alone would be worth it.

Apologizing for business decisions that were wrong or didn't turn out as well as you had hoped may seem counterproductive to you, but it isn't.

It's just counterintuitive. Most of your business associates might expect you to attach blame elsewhere or to cover over the wrong decision in some way. But when you do the bigger thing by taking responsibility and saying, "I honestly thought that was a good decision, but I was wrong," your stock will go up immensely with your bosses, coworkers, clients, and other business associates.

Whether in military campaigns or business, victory usually comes to the person who is willing to do the unexpected, to do something different, perhaps something that has never been done before. To the victor go the spoils, they say, but victory usually goes to the entrepreneur who is creative and gutsy enough to initiate a bold, imaginative plan. Think of most of the top business executives you know; in almost every case, you will find innovative, counterintuitive men and women. They don't do things the way everyone else does. They refuse to conform to the status quo, and they are hugely successful as a result.

Knockout Entrepreneurs don't always go with the flow. They have the courage to do things differently, yet to be humble and teachable while doing so. They are willing to admit when they've made mistakes, and even more importantly they are willing to do everything possible to make things right. Even in the face of difficulty, adversity, or tough economic times, a Knockout Entrepreneur continues to have faith and to believe for a great future.

KNOCKOUT IDEAS
TO STIMULATE YOUR SUCCESS

1. Everyone knows that it is foolish and futile to keep doing the same thing again and again and expect different results. A radical change in the direction of your life may require you to take some counterintuitive

steps. Consider ways that you can go against the flow in your endeavors.

2. Remember, changing your life demands changing your will. Thinking about it is not enough; you must take specific, productive actions. Will you remain as you are today, or have you resolved to make the necessary changes? What three areas in your life need the most work right now?

3. Thinking has gone out of fashion. Most people say, "I don't have time to think; I have too much to do!" But if you are going to break with the status quo, the place to start is in your mind. Set aside five to ten minutes each day this week to do nothing else but think. Stop everything else; don't try to think while you work or think while you drive. Close your eyes, focus, and think of the areas you hope to change. This may be the most productive time in your week.

CHAPTER SEVEN

DEAL BREAKERS—BE WILLING TO WALK AWAY

I once had an opportunity to work with a company that wanted to develop the George Foreman Restaurant chain. They offered me a ton of money, and I was ready to sign my name on the dotted line until I found out that they were planning to serve alcohol at the restaurants. Now, understand, if you want to drink alcohol, that's your business, but I don't drink, and I have worked real hard at maintaining a positive image so I can be a role model for young people, especially the inner-city kids of Houston who come to the George Foreman Youth and Community Center. What would they think if they went to a George Foreman Restaurant and saw people drinking alcohol? It would be inconsistent with who I am.

When I expressed my concerns to the restaurant developers, they understood and appreciated my position, but they said, "George, nowadays, it is almost impossible for a restaurant chain to survive without selling alcohol. People like to have a drink before dinner or while they are watching the ball game. We must have alcohol in the deal."

"Nope, not if you want to put my name above the door," I stated firmly.

The developers went away disappointed, but then they came back with another idea: "Look, George, here's what we'll do. We'll build the restaurant known as the George Foreman Restaurant, but we'll put the bar right beside it, on the far side of the building, so it is almost a separate entity from the food service area. And since you don't want any proceeds from alcohol sales, we will donate a percentage of the proceeds each year to the George Foreman Youth and Community Center. We figure that ought to be about a million dollars each year that we will donate to the youth center."

"A million dollars a year donated to the youth center?"

"That's right," the developers said with a smile. "And you won't be selling a drop of alcohol, but it will be right next door."

"No deal," I said. "I'm sorry, I just can't do that. I'd like to have a million dollars a year for my kids at the youth center, but those kids don't need money. They need me. And they need me to be a man of integrity that they can trust and look to as an example of a man they want to emulate."

The money was there; the marketing plan was in place. All I had to do was sign the contract and not only would I be richer, but the kids at the George Foreman Youth and Community Center would benefit as well. As much as I tried to explain to the developers, they couldn't imagine someone walking away from a multimillion-dollar deal because of alcohol. But to me the deal breaker wasn't just about the alcohol; it was about my personal integrity.

You never draw lines when it comes to love—you don't want any ultimatums in your relationships: "If she ever does this, I'm out of here." "If he ever does that, I'm gone." Instead, if he or she crosses a line, draw another line.

Certainly you should never put yourself or your family members in danger, but keep drawing those lines until you can't draw anymore.

In business, however, you must draw firm, immovable, impenetrable lines when it comes to maintaining your integrity. Anything that might cause me to cross one of those lines is what I call a deal breaker. It's an issue that can cause the best deal to fall apart.

Draw those lines, and don't cross them. In business and in life know your deal breakers before you enter negotiations. Ponder the things that really matter to you in life as well as in a business deal; often these matters come back to integrity issues. Being honest and fair, maintaining your reputation, creating an excellent product that you have confidence in and you know can do the job or perform properly when the public uses it—these are the lines that matter.

Regardless of what product you sell or service you offer, your main ingredient is your personal integrity. Without integrity you will fail before you start. Being truly successful is being able to look in the mirror and say, "I still like myself. I like who I am and the way I conduct my life. It may have cost me some money, but that was a good decision, and I'm glad that I made it."

I've never regretted acting on that deal breaker and walking away, and God has brought numerous opportunities across my path to replace that deal that would have compromised my integrity. Even as I write these pages, I'm considering another George Foreman Restaurant, but without alcohol. You don't lose when you do what is right for the largest number of people. The Bible teaches you to count the cost when you build a house. I counted that cost before I walked away from the restaurant deal that would include serving alcohol.

And as for a restaurant not being able to survive without alcohol, just think of McDonald's and Chick-fil-A. They are some of the most successful restaurants in history, and they don't serve alcohol. Moreover, Chick-fil-A doesn't open on Sundays. At the same time, dozens of high-profile celebrity restaurants have gone under. Why? Because they were all about being glitzy and glittery rather than providing a great product for the public. All too often the owners went into the business strictly to make money rather than to develop a great product at a great price that people would feel good about returning to again and again. But when people find a restaurant with great food, great service, and great prices, they will patronize it, promote it, and help it to stay profitable.

One of the products with which I have been involved is George Foreman's Knock-Out Cleaner, and more recently George Foreman's Knock-Out Pro Green products. I've had numerous opportunities to endorse other cleaning products, and I've turned down enormous amounts of money because some of those products were not good for our environment. I'm always looking for excellent, safe, environmentally friendly products that we can include in the Knock-Out Cleaner line. If a product bears the label "Keep out of the reach of children," that's probably telling us that the product may not be as safe as we'd like it to be. On the other hand, products that enhance a healthy lifestyle pique my interest.

I believe we all have a responsibility to take good care of God's creation. It is not Mother Nature or Father Time whom we are going to stand before to give an account one day regarding what we did with God's gift of this earth. Almighty God Himself will examine our books on that day. I want my record to be spotless, and if my cleaning products can't clean a floor or an article of clothing without smearing my record before God, then those products aren't for me.

DON'T SET YOUR STANDARDS BY THE SCOUNDRELS

Will you encounter shysters and scoundrels in business? Sure you will. In every profession you can find men and women willing to lie, cheat, steal, or worse. Most doctors, for example, operate by their Hippocratic oath and do all they can to help their patients. Occasionally, though, you will hear of a doctor who does the minimum necessary or may even use his skills to hurt someone. That doesn't tarnish the entire profession of medicine.

Similarly you sometimes hear of professional athletes, movie stars, or other entertainers who have gone bad, or politicians who decided to line their pockets rather than represent the public well. No question about it—their poor examples hurt the image of the entire field, but you don't have to emulate their despicable conduct. Find what is good about them, and appreciate that.

Unfortunately, the world will always be quick to point out the preacher who rips off his congregation or the entrepreneur who purposely sold a defective product. But that doesn't mean you need to be one of those charlatans. Sadly, rip-offs happen; deceivers lie; crooks cheat. Commit yourself to the pledge "That won't ever happen through me." Never lower your standards or compromise your integrity to make a deal.

Before you start negotiating any deal, here are a few other things to keep in mind: be prepared and know your weaknesses; more important, know when to walk away. But how do you identify when giving up on a deal is the right thing to do? Too often, many people throw in the towel because they are scared or intimidated. Other people are quitters; they don't like confrontations of any kind, so they acquiesce or compromise their integrity just to keep the peace.

A good fighter knows there are times to throw in the towel, especially when given advice by trusted cornermen, the ring doctor, the referee, or other friends or objective observers who have your best interests at heart and are not easily overwhelmed by your fighting spirit. If they advise you to walk away, they can see that you are in danger of suffering injury or perhaps a potentially career-ending trauma. That's why it is all the more important to keep good people around you, so when you are having trouble seeing the issues clearly, they can be your "eyes." Remember, there is no shame in walking away from a deal if it allows you to fight another day.

Don't burn yourself out, using up all your options in the first couple rounds of negotiations. In boxing, quite often nothing of significance occurs during the first round. Oh sure, occasionally you will see a dramatic first-round knockout, but that is the rarity rather than the norm. Usually the fighters are scoping each other out during the early stages of the match; they are testing each other, looking for weaknesses they can exploit or opportunities of which they can take advantage. Sooner or later somebody will throw the first hard punch, a potentially match-winning blow.

If at all possible in your negotiating process, attempt to throw the "first punch." You can't win unless you are in the fight, and you are not really in the fight until you have staked out some territory. Once you have thrown your first few punches, you will have a much better idea of how the negotiations are going to go, where the opportunities and pitfalls lie, and where you need to adjust and amend your game plan.

Whether you are negotiating in marriage or your career, with a banker or a service provider, pay close attention to the other person's responses. Observe body language and eye contact. Notice how he reacts to your opening forays. Don't go for a knockout when all you need is a series of strong points. Don't be discouraged if events or relationships proceed slowly; you will have more time to assess your position.

Keep in mind that encountering a few problems does not necessarily mean you have hit a deal breaker. Problems are a part of life; working through snags, pits, and potholes is a part of every negotiation process, so don't give up easily and don't give up too soon on a good idea.

When problems arise, you will usually find two types of people: whiners and winners. Whiners obstruct progress; they spend hours complaining about this point or that, without offering positive solutions. Winners acknowledge the existence of the problem, but they try to offer practical ideas that can help resolve the matter in a manner that is satisfactory to both parties.

COMMUNICATION IS THE KEY

One of the main reasons so many potentially good deals fall apart during the negotiating process is a failure to communicate. Your personal and professional success will be determined largely by your ability to convey your ideas clearly to another person.

"Oh, George, I'm not a public speaker," I hear you saying. "I don't even like to talk in front of a group."

I understand, and you are not alone. As a matter of fact, speaking in public always ranks as one of the top fears for most people, right below being bit by a rattlesnake! But if you want to be a success, you must learn to communicate your ideas, and for most of us, that includes presenting those ideas in public.

To help you avoid missing an opportunity to close a deal because of poor communication, allow me to give you some simple tips that have worked for me. First of all, be prepared—know your stuff. If you have a lot of statistics and specific details, you may find it helpful to prepare a handout for the other person or group to whom you are presenting your ideas. Think through what you are going to say, and rehearse the conversation in your mind before you get into negotiations. If possible, practice your presentation with a friend or coworker and ask that person to give you honest feedback for ways to improve.

Speak in a relaxed, natural, conversational tone, as if you are speaking with a friend. Use words that are comfortable and familiar to you rather than trying to impress someone with big words you may not understand or really feel. Let your face help you do your talking by radiating warmth, sincerity, enthusiasm, and conviction. Vary your speaking pattern, so you aren't talking in a boring monotone. Speak in a clear, firm, but friendly voice, not too loud but not so soft that you come across as weak or uncertain of your facts or position.

An intentional pause can often be dramatic, but unnecessary pauses can be distracting or downright irritating. Develop the habit of speaking without empty phrases and wishy-washy pauses such as "ahhh," "ummm," "like" and "well, you know" that make you sound insecure or lacking in confidence or competence. You'd do better to state your case in simple, clear sentences than to speak haltingly.

No matter how fantastic your ideas may be, they will remain yours alone unless you communicate them to others. You do not necessarily communicate merely because you are talking; to communicate you must impart your information or ideas, and the people listening must understand what you mean. It is not enough to lay your ideas on the table or to speak your mind. You must be aware of—and sensitive to—the questions, feelings, or objections your words are evoking. Try to answer those questions as you speak and you will discover that you are getting much better results in your negotiations.

Whether you are speaking to an audience of one or one thousand, maintain eye contact. Don't simply stare at your notes; if possible, know your material well enough that you can avoid looking at your notes any more than absolutely necessary. Especially in a small gathering, look people directly in the eyes as you are talking. Have you ever talked to a person who, while supposedly engaged in conversation with you, was looking over your shoulder, checking or sending e-mail, or glancing around the room at someone else? Frustrating, isn't it? You almost want to say, "Am I keeping you from something?"

To avoid that particular chronic crime of poor communication, maintain eye contact as much as possible with the people to whom you are speaking. When someone else in the room is talking, let the person know you are listening by looking him or her in the eyes. Occasionally nod your head or offer other indicators to show that you are listening. If appropriate, inject comments such as, "Oh?" "Really?" "Tell me more," and "How does that work?"

Avoid being a passive negotiator. Nobody talks to doormats for long, so interact verbally. Pick up on any verbal clues the other person gives you and pursue them.

Ask questions, especially ones that cannot be answered with a simple yes or no, and then reiterate the other person's answers so you can be sure you heard and understood the person correctly. Say things such as, "As I understand what you are saying, you intend to do such and such. Did I understand you correctly?" Then give the other person an opportunity to respond and to clarify any confusion.

You may be negotiating a deal to offer your services or products to a company, but always remember that you are dealing with a person. In this regard, sales trainer Brian Tracy suggests:

Ask questions about what the person does and what results he is responsible for. What are the key performance indicators of his job? What does she get paid for? What results is he expected to achieve for the company? How is she appraised or evaluated by her superiors? These are key questions to ask and find out the answers for . . . people always seek improvement in their conditions. They will only take action on an offer if they feel that they will be better off as a result. In business organizations, people will only approve the purchase of a product or service if they feel that it will improve their personal positions in the organization.[1]

Focus on the benefits that the person with whom you are negotiating will receive personally, and your chances of closing the deal with the business or company will be much higher.

If you will be speaking to larger audiences, you may want to sharpen your speaking skills by hiring a speaking coach or joining a local group such as Toastmasters to help you become more comfortable with public speaking. You can also learn a lot about your speaking style by recording your talk or, better yet, using a video recorder to study your mannerisms and your vocal performance. As you see and hear yourself as others do (or will), you can correct bad habits and work on your communication skills.

Remember, successful people are the masters of their words. They do not allow their words to master them. They know that to achieve their goals, they must speak the truth with confidence, more often using words of acceptance than rejection. Have you ever noticed that every word you say creates an effect, either positively or negatively, on the people who hear you? Your words can be the glue that holds things together or the dynamite that blows them apart. If at all possible, avoid negative statements to or about another person. Words are powerful. Marriages have both been sealed and destroyed because of words. Wars are sometimes won or lost as a result of words. And deals are often made or broken because of those powerful little puffs of air that come out of our mouths.

When you are negotiating, make an effort to say something appreciative to everyone with whom you are dealing. Be truthful in all your statements, and make it your intention to encourage or uplift the person with whom you are interacting. You will be amazed how much more effective your negotiations become.

If you hit an impasse, try to briefly change the subject, and say something positive to the person with whom you are dealing. If the wall is still there when you come back to the negotiations, take a short break. Get up, walk away from the conversation for a few minutes, and then come back and try again. Sometimes the best thing you can do while negotiating is to remain thoughtful and silent for a few minutes, allowing the person to wonder what you are mulling over in your mind. If after every effort to resolve the issue that is keeping you apart proves futile, you may need to clearly state, "This is a potential deal breaker for me," and then proceed accordingly from there.

TAKE YOUR TIME

Some people say, "Don't sweat the small stuff." I don't believe that. Knockout Entrepreneurs are proactive; they look for small things that can be improved; they seek to address problems when they are small and can be dealt with decisively and with relative ease, before things get out of hand. The difference, of course, is that Knockout Entrepreneurs don't mind the work or the heat causing them to sweat.

One key to avoiding a deal breaker is defining the problem as simply as possible. Every problem has two basic elements that must be considered: Why is it a problem? How can it be solved? It may seem silly, but a lot of conflicts in business stem from fuzzy, undefined issues. Many times a solution will appear, seemingly out of thin air, after the real problem is identified and the facts are examined. Look for the simplest solution to every problem, clearing away as much clutter as possible, and then lay out a step-by-step plan for implementing the solution.

Take your time; don't rush into anything or out of anything. Be willing to walk away from a deal at any point, but don't be too hasty to do so. Stay calm and deliberate in your dealings. There's no need to rush or to get frazzled or desperate. Your greatest assets in negotiating will be a clear head and a calm spirit. Panic clouds the mind and paralyzes the will, making it next to impossible to solve problems wisely. The old saying "Haste makes waste" is usually true.

Most panic-driven solutions end up costing you more in time, energy, resources, and money, so take your time. If necessary, say, "Let's come back to this issue tomorrow." Go home, sleep on it, allow your mind to be refreshed, ask the good Lord above for some insight and guidance, and perhaps the dawning of a new day will bring with it fresh ideas for solving the problem.

Consider the people with whom you might be working, and decide whether you are a good match for each other. Do you have similar values? Are your goals and ambitions compatible? Are there areas in the relationship or factors in the deal about which you feel reticent or uncomfortable? Again, don't rush; take your time. Rarely will you lose a deal because you took too much time; more often you will get into trouble or make a poor decision because you got in too big of a hurry to close the deal. Remember, if it is not a win-win for everyone involved, don't do the deal.

Have I missed out on a few opportunities that I wish I had gotten involved with? Oh sure. Every successful person misses a few shots here and there. But I've also talked with too many people who said, "Oh, George, you made the right decision. It's a good thing you didn't get involved in that deal. We did, and it turned out that the venture was not credible."

Always give yourself enough time to think through and evaluate the positives and negatives of a deal, but never allow yourself to get into a situation where you cannot walk away. Most likely you will need to learn how to say no more often.

KEEP YOUR WORD

If you choose to move ahead with a deal, always keep your agreements. Anytime that you break a contract, whether written or verbal, you lose the respect and trust of others. If you don't keep your agreements, regardless of the reason, you will lose credibility. That's why you should enter only those agreements that you absolutely intend to keep.

If circumstances beyond your control occur—really beyond your control, not simply that you don't feel well or a better opportunity arises—notify the other party immediately. It doesn't matter whether your computer crashes, your car won't start, you are snowed in and can't get to work, you missed a deadline, or something else happens over which you had little to no control. Allow the other party the option of canceling the deal or deciding whether to continue to use your services. Clean up any loose ends, and do your best to lessen the damage. Don't blame anyone else or try to justify yourself. Do your best to restore your credibility every way you can.

Deal breakers happen, so you must learn when and how to walk away, but if you enter into the deal, you must do your best to make it work. You'll have some extra bounce in your step when you know that you've done the right thing. Remember, if the deal isn't good for all the interested parties, if it is not a win-win situation, it's not the kind of deal a Knockout Entrepreneur gets involved in.

KNOCKOUT IDEAS
TO STIMULATE YOUR SUCCESS

1. "Know thyself" is a bit of ageless advice we should all take to heart, especially before entering into negotiations with someone. What really matters to you in life?

2. Probably no skill is more important to your success as a negotiator than your ability to communicate. Communication is not simply stating your position or using a batch of big words to impress your

listeners. Communication is getting your ideas across to your audience in a way they understand. Think of a time when conflict occurred in your office, home, or group because of a communication failure on somebody's part. What would you do differently?

3. We often communicate more with our appearance and body language than we do with our words. Ask a close friend, mentor, or pastor, somebody who is willing to be honest with you, "What signals am I sending out through my nonverbal communication?"

CHAPTER EIGHT

YOU GOTTA MAKE 'EM LOVE YA!

ce cream! I got ice cream!" I can still hear my dad telling stories about a street vendor who sold ice cream and other products in our old neighborhood. We never really knew his name; we just called him "Mr. Ice Cream." Each day Mr. Ice Cream peddled his products up and down our street, calling out his specials of the day. "I got ice cream! I got fresh tomatoes! I got watermelons, three for a dollar!" He was a handsome fellow with a perpetual, friendly smile. He was always dressed neatly and was the picture of integrity. Nobody had a bad story about Mr. Ice Cream. Nobody ever complained that Mr. Ice Cream had ripped them off or sold an inferior product, or that he had spoken inappropriately. No, Mr. Ice Cream handled his business and his personal life with honesty and always acted in a manner above reproach.

He put on an enthusiastic little show as he made his way up and down the street, and his happy, exuberant personality made people want to watch and listen to what he had to say. And they always noticed the products he had to sell and they usually bought something from him. People loved to see Mr. Ice Cream coming up the street. Whether they needed what he was selling or not, they came out to enjoy the show. He was his own best advertising campaign with the unspoken motto "You gotta make 'em love ya!"

An interviewer once asked me to describe the way I liked to do business. That was an easy question for me. "Make them love you!" I responded with a smile. "If they love you, they'll always buy you."

In fact, when the George Foreman grill first debuted, it wasn't exactly flying off the shelves in department stores. It was being *shoved* off the department store shelves in favor of other products because the grill just wasn't selling. About that time I went on QVC to promote the product. My model for my appearance on QVC was Mr. Ice Cream. "I got this fantastic grill! I got hamburgers! Juicy hamburgers. Mmmm-mmm, is this burger ever good!" I basically put on my own version of the Mr. Ice Cream show. The grills began to move—and they've been moving ever since!

The other principle I've incorporated from Mr. Ice Cream is to "always be nice." You can be a successful businessperson and still be nice. That's one reason why I smile so much. Someone has said that the most destitute person in the world is a person without a smile. I agree.

Being nice doesn't mean you are a pushover in business. Far from it! It means that you like who you are, that you sincerely enjoy helping other people, and one of the ways you can do that is by providing them with your product or service in a most congenial manner. Give people a smile and more than their money's worth, and they will keep coming back to you again and again.

The nicest human being can outsell anyone! All you need is a good product and a sincere salesperson. Think back to when Mr. Coffee fast-brewing coffee machines first came out. The company hired retired major league baseball great Joe DiMaggio to represent the product in commercials. Joe *looked* like Mr. Coffee! His sophisticated yet friendly appearance exuded confidence and integrity. Consequently the public bought Mr. Coffee machines by the millions. Was it a good product at a good price that met a need? Oh yes. But Joe was the likable person who sold it to us. We weren't merely buying a coffee machine; we were buying Joe.

Or consider the phenomenal success of the online matchmaking service eHarmony.com. Much of the company's fantastic success, especially in the early years as the company was getting off the ground, was due to the confidence evoking image of Dr. Neil Clark Warren, the grandfatherly looking psychologist who founded the company and appeared in all the early television and radio commercials. Conservative, yet relaxed and approachable in his plaid sports coat, blue dress shirt, and sedate tie, Dr. Warren's appearance was reassuring to a single person thinking, *This guy can really help me find my soul mate for life.* Millions of men and women turned to him to help them find their ideal marriage partners, and many found exactly the person for whom they were best suited.

Maybe you will never advertise on television, but you may take out an ad in a local newspaper or magazine. When you are ready to advertise your products—especially on television—be sure the person pitching your product looks trustworthy and sincere. Intelligence is not the paramount issue; your success depends on the image you present. While people may admire intellectually brilliant people, they don't usually feel comfortable spending a lot of time with them. If you succeed in business, it won't be merely because people think you are smart; it will be because people like you, trust you, and believe that you like them and care about them.

Smile—even when things aren't going so well, or your circumstances are less than cheerful. Take an interest in the client or customer. Instead of concerning yourself with how each new client can assist you, ask each person,

"How can I help you?" Sincere questions such as, "What can I do for you?" will set you apart from most of your competitors.

BUILD RELATIONSHIPS

A few careers may require you to be an introvert if you want to be successful, but in most cases, to get ahead in life, you have to talk to people about your product or service—at every opportunity with enthusiasm. If you don't believe in what you are selling and aren't excited about it, why should anyone else buy it? Socialize in your community, meet people, go to functions, and talk about your product everywhere. For instance, I'm on the Board of Regents at Pepperdine University. I enjoy meeting the outstanding, successful people who are on that board, and of course, I enjoy talking with them about their businesses. Inevitably, as I take an interest in their businesses, they take an interest in mine. I learn a great deal from them too, and I implement some of the ideas they share with me.

I try to build a relationship with every person I meet, even if our meeting is only a matter of seconds. I look the person in the eyes, shake hands, smile, and try to say something kind. I enjoy having fun with him, especially a young person. From then on, every time that person sees my picture on a product, he is reminded that we are friends. Even if he doesn't buy what I'm selling, I believe that my new friend will at least consider what I have to say.

DROP THE KILLER INSTINCT

You can be successful in business without having a killer instinct. When I came back during my second career in boxing, I didn't have that killer attitude, but I had a goal and I was motivated to achieve it. When I was younger, my only goal was to win and to be mean.

In my younger years, boxing was a popular sport and all the great boxers had nicknames and some sort of image, a reputation that was tagged on them (often by their promoters). For example, there were "Smokin' " Joe Frazier and the social folk hero Muhammad Ali. Sugar Ray Robinson was known as the "Sweet Science Man." Me? I decided I would label myself as the "World's Most Dangerous Fighter."

Especially after I lost the fight to Muhammad Ali, I became even more obsessed with putting up a tough guy image. Everybody had something that said, "I'm tough." Even their dogs were tough! A number of boxers owned Dobermans and pit bulls. There were athletes in other sports who were always seen with their snarling German shepherds. The Dallas Cowboys had a real cowboy who did rodeo bulldogging, chasing down a steer while riding a horse, roping the fleeing steer, wrestling it to the ground, and tying its legs. That was tough!

So I had to be tougher. "I'll show them who is the meanest man of all," I said. To do so, I decided to purchase a live lion as a pet. Then to take it a step further, I went out and bought a tiger and kept both animals at my ranch. The word quickly got around among my competitors (not to mention my neighbors), "Man, that George Foreman is crazy! He walks around his ranch with a lion and a tiger. George isn't afraid of anyone or anything! Don't mess with George Foreman."

I loved it when I heard those comments. I wanted to be feared, especially since the loss to Ali had taken me down a notch in the boxing public's eyes. I felt that I needed to rebuild my tough guy image. I did all sorts of foolish things trying to bolster that tough persona.

For instance, when *People* magazine first appeared on the publishing scene in 1974, the editor called and wanted to do a feature story about me in one of the early issues. My public relations man, Bill Caplan, and I thought it would be a great opportunity. "Let me show the people that I am so strong, they will realize that I must have been robbed in Africa in that fight against Ali. Let's show them how strong I really am!" I said. We bought a cow from one of my neighbors in Livermore, California, where my first ranch was located. Our plan was to stage a photo shoot with me holding a full-grown cow on my shoulders!

But as anyone who has ever done a photo shoot knows, things aren't always as they seem. To get a great shot, photographers might spend hours getting the background just right, setting the lights in the perfect angles, and adjusting a myriad of other little details that will drive you bonkers if you are in a hurry—or if you happen to be holding a live cow on your shoulders. To make matters much easier, we had six strong guys who were going to help me hoist the cow onto my shoulders and then help to hold the animal in place until the photographer got the photo he wanted. After the shot, Bill and the photographer would cut the six guys out of the picture so it would appear that I was holding the heavy cow all by myself.

We all gathered at the ranch, the photographer was finally ready, and the guys and I prepared to pick up the cow. But as we were picking up the big bovine, with me under the cow in the middle, two of the guys slipped and fell. When the other guys saw the two men fall down, they suddenly backed off too, and there I was, holding a cow on my shoulders and back—all by myself!

"He did it for real!" one of the men shouted as the photographer rapidly snapped picture after picture. There is no easy way to extricate yourself from under a live cow, so I was walking around the pasture with that cow on top of me. It was almost easier to hold the animal up in the air than it was to let it down!

The photograph did indeed appear in the magazine, and my friends and enemies in the boxing world went wild. "George Foreman carried a live cow on his shoulders!" they crowed. Others picked up on the point that I wanted to make: "Something must have been really wrong with George when he fought Ali in Africa. I mean, the man can carry a cow! Surely he was strong enough to have beaten Muhammad Ali."

Still looking for ever more outlandish ways to show that I was mean and tough, I went to Canada in 1975 to fight five men in one night. I boxed each man three rounds and beat all five of them. It was a crazy thing to do, but to tell you the truth, I was a bit unhinged during that period of my life. I was consumed with anger against Muhammad Ali, and all I could think about was getting another shot at him. In fact, *Sports Illustrated* did a cover story on me in the December 15, 1975, issue, with a ferocious-looking picture of me on the cover and the title "I Want Ali Again."

The message was getting out: nobody could beat me fair and square. After all, George Foreman had the heart of a lion and the cunning skill of the tiger. And I did! I raised those two big cats from cubs. I loved them, played with them, and roughhoused with them—and I trusted them. The tiger weighed close to four hundred pounds, and the lion weighed even more.

ABC Sports came to my ranch to film me before an upcoming boxing match, and I used the tiger and the lion in the interview. The sports guys were scared to death, but they loved it or at least pretended they did. But when it was time to put the cats in their dens, my older brother Robert took a chain and began tugging on the lion. The lion turned on Robert and attacked him. I saw what was happening and stepped in to protect my brother, but the big cat continued his attack. He wanted my brother, but he came at me with a speed faster than any knockout punch I'd ever seen. I knew I had to do something quickly before either Robert or I was dead, so I threw my fist toward the lion's head as hard as I could.

Lions are not only large and strong; they are also extremely agile and quick. The lion dodged the punch better than any man I'd ever fought. I missed him completely, whirled around, and almost fell to the ground. The lion could have attacked me right there, but he didn't. As strange as it might seem, I think that lion somehow realized that I was not going to back down from him, that I was willing to protect my brother with my life. When the lion found out that I wasn't afraid of him (good thing he couldn't hear my pounding heart!), he backed away and turned toward his cage.

That was one of the most frightening things ever to happen to me. I never played with that lion again after that day, although I kept him at the ranch for a while. The tiger was tough too, but the only time he was tempted to attack was when I turned my back on him.

I loved having those animals nearby, and they did achieve the purpose for which I originally purchased them. They reinforced the image that George Foreman was one tough fellow. But after that frightening encounter, I never looked at those animals the same way. I noticed that whenever I'd bring the children around to look at the lion and the tiger, the cats seemed to fix their eyes on the kids. That scared me. I knew those animals, and I knew I could no longer trust them.

A couple of years later I found the good Lord. When I committed my life to Him, suddenly I realized there was no reason to prove anything to anybody. As a matter of fact, rather than show how tough I was, I preferred to show a different side of me, the new George, you might say. A George Foreman who smiled, who loved, who still competed hard, but a George Foreman whom no one ever again would have to fear.

Considering my uneasiness about the cats and the joy of my new life, I began looking for an opportunity to give them away, but I wanted to find a good home for them. A man in New Jersey promised to keep the lion and the tiger together—that was important to me because I knew the cats loved each other. Those cats then belonged to a different world, one in which people did not use them as a symbol of their toughness, where they were kept as specimens to be respected, cared for, and given a little dignity.

They say that animals take on the personality of their owners, and I think that is true. Nowadays, no matter how big a dog I get, all he or she ever wants to do is lick me to death!

My point is that you don't have to be mean and nasty to win at business. You can compete aggressively without trying to destroy your competitors. I know some highly visible businesspeople will say the opposite; they think that to succeed in business or in your career, you need to be ruthless to get what you want. They believe you have to constantly watch out for number one—yourself—and you should hit the competition hard and often. To them, all's fair in love and war, in pursuing your career and getting more for yourself. If it means that someone else must be trampled or hurt so you can get ahead, well, so be it.

I respectfully disagree. I believe you can be kind and still be successful. You can be ambitious and diligent without being greedy. You shouldn't have to hurt other people to get what you want in life, and if you do, maybe what you want isn't worth having.

I know what it feels like to hurt someone to get what I wanted. Boxing as a younger man, I balled my fists as tight as I could when I hit my opponents because I wanted to hurt them. I viewed them as animals to be hunted. My opponents weren't human beings—they were the enemy. As I stood in the ring and glared at the other fighter, I'd think, *I'm going to kill him.*

A NEW WAY OF DOING BUSINESS

When I decided to get back into the sport after I'd met the good Lord, I learned a new way to box—without hate. During my comeback to win the championship again, I never threw one punch in anger. Instead of tightening my fist into a ball, I never completely closed up my hand. I knew I couldn't seriously hurt anyone if my fist wasn't tight. In boxing, like any sport, you can control what you do. I never injured anyone in any of my matches during my second career in boxing.

Sometimes I got booed during my comeback because I didn't display that killer instinct and I wouldn't destroy my opponents as I had done in the matches of my earlier years. In my fight against Dwight Muhammad Qawi in Las Vegas, I heard some spectators yell, "Get tough, George!" I found out later they wanted a fast knockout because they had bet on the rounds. They weren't encouraging me; they were hoping to get easy money.

Before I fought Evander Holyfield, I had a dream that I killed him in the ring. When I fought him a few days later for the championship, I stunned him with a punch, and he stumbled toward me and held on to me. The old George would have finished him off right then. But as soon as he grabbed me, the dream popped into my mind. I was afraid that if I hit him again at that point, I might truly hurt him, and I knew that I would regret it. So I let him hold on for a moment until he could clear his head. I ended up losing the championship bout on points, but I walked away holding my head high. I was prepared to lose the championship fight rather than hurt Evander and have that awful dream come true.

One of my favorite Bible verses is "Blessed are the meek, for they shall inherit the earth."[1] Not that they will *conquer* the earth, but that they will *inherit* it. It isn't necessary to destroy another person's business, career, relationships, or reputation so you can succeed. You don't have to coerce, steal, or cheat to get what you want. Do it God's way, and you'll inherit it.

Many kids come into my youth center wanting to be boxers. I teach them: "Never throw a punch in anger. This is an honorable sport; it's been around for thousands of years. You don't have to hurt anyone. You don't need a killer instinct to win."

VICTORY OUT OF DEFEAT

But sometimes even when you lose, you still win. Not long after the fight with Evander Holyfield, I received two airline tickets in the mail. A group of friends had traveled all the way from Austria to attend my bout with Evander in Atlantic City and to cheer me on. I hadn't even known they were there until after the fight. I met these men when I was invited to Austria in 1990. I love Austria, and I still had quite a number of fans there from my former championship boxing career as well as my newfound friends who took an interest in my comeback career. In Austria, my hosts treated me like a king. I toured the countryside, ate the best food, and attended a concert with the famous Vienna Boys' Choir. Those boys can sing!

My last stop in Austria was at the Spanish Riding School, where the world-famous Royal Lipizzaner stallions are housed and trained and where they perform. And what a performance it is! The Lipizzaners are a gorgeous breed of horse, known for their leaping and kicking abilities—soaring through the air with their front legs tucked neatly under their chests, with their back legs propelling them high into the leap. Their abilities to perform incredibly graceful maneuvers are truly astounding, considering how big they are. I loved those horses the moment I saw them! The Lipizzaners usually are born brown, but as they grow up, they turn lighter. Many of them turn almost pure white. These are the horses you usually see performing in the shows, with their trainers and handlers decked out in handsome equestrian outfits.

The Lipizzaners have an interesting history. They were nearly wiped out during World War II and probably would be extinct today had it not been for General George Patton and the heroic efforts of the Forty-second Squadron of the United States Army's Second Calvary. Near the end of the war, Vienna was under attack by Allied bombers. Colonel Alois Podhajsky, head of the Spanish Riding School in Vienna, feared that the valuable Lipizzaner stallions would be destroyed by either the bombing raids or the vicious ground fighting as the German armies made their last stands against the advancing Allied troops. The colonel moved the stallions by train to St. Martin's in upper Austria, about two hundred miles away. Along the way, starving war refugees tried to steal the horses for food, but the colonel managed to get them safely to an estate owned by a friend.

When US forces moved in to St. Martin's, an officer recognized Podhajsky and the horses and sent word to General Patton. George Patton and Podhajsky were acquainted, having competed in equestrian events during the prewar Olympics. Patton's forces rescued more than 150 Lipizzaners and moved them to safety. Eventually they were reunited with the Spanish Riding School, where they continued to perform when they weren't appearing in shows around the world.

My hosts in Austria had arranged for me to sit right up front on the ground level to watch these aristocratic-looking white stallions perform. I was in awe as I watched them leap through the air with such ease. I could hardly believe my eyes when they did pirouettes by balancing on their hind legs and pivoting a half or full circle before coming down on all fours, all in perfect precision. It was clear that the horse trainers loved their animals, and that the horses were not responding to viciousness; they were performing incredible feats, seemingly the impossible, in response to the love and care lavished on them by their trainers. Certainly they were well disciplined, but the discipline was always couched in love. The horses had a powerful connection with their trainers.

In your business or in your close relationships, if you want people to perform Herculean feats on your behalf, they must know that you care about them. Oh yes, they will respond to training and discipline, but you will draw far more out of them if they know you sincerely care about them as people, not simply employees or coworkers.

The same is true of your customers or clients. In his book *What Customers Really Want*, Scott McKain contends that "customers desire a connection with the people and the organizations with whom they do business so the outcome is a compelling experience that transcends mere transactions. They want to feel as if you care for them. . . . They want to believe that you worry as much about them as you do their business."[2] If you provide your clients that sort of experience, their loyalty to you will be almost unbreakable. They will do more for you than you could ever dare ask.

At one point during the Lipizzaner show, I leaned over to one of my Austrian hosts and asked, "How can I buy one of these horses? How much? Who can I contact to transport one of these beauties to Texas?"

My hosts laughed, and one of them said, "Look, George. If you beat Evander Holyfield, we'll *give* you one of the horses!" We all laughed, and I didn't think much more about it until I saw my friends in Atlantic City after the fight.

That bout with Evander had gotten rather tough, and at times it could have gone either way. The crowd was on its feet almost the entire fight, with some people standing on chairs, I later heard. But even though I lost the fight on points, those men from Austria were so impressed with my efforts, they decided to give me a stallion anyhow!

They sent plane tickets for my wife and me to return to Austria to pick out the stallion we wanted. A few years later we were given a filly and that was the beginning of my herd of Royal Lipizzaner stallions that I keep on my ranch in Texas to this day. I don't sell the horses; I don't even show them at equestrian events. I just love them, and I'm proud to have a small part in keeping their great lineage going. I used to ride the stallion at least once a year, on January 10, my birthday. When you ride one of those animals, you have to be ready for a fight. Talk about strong willed! Occasionally the stallion would drop me, so my wife doesn't like me to ride him too much anymore. But I still take special care of the horses. The way I figure, if I keep my herd healthy, someone like General Patton might have need of them someday!

If you want your family, coworkers, or friends to do above and beyond what is expected, you gotta make them love you, and you gotta let them know that you love them and that you will go the extra mile to see them succeed and perform feats of greatness.

WORK SMARTER

My skills as an older boxer definitely weren't the same as when I was younger, so I had to fight smarter. Instead of relying on my physical power, I concentrated on mental power, searching for the weaknesses in my opponents, and I usually found some. Similarly, I had lost a lot of speed and quickness, which forced me to train differently. Instead of training for power by pounding the punching bag longer and harder, I trained for endurance. I worked hard to get back into shape, starting by running short distances and gradually increasing my stamina. I got to the point that on most days I ran ten, fifteen, or seventeen miles.

When I boxed in my younger years, I usually knocked out my opponents in the early rounds of the match, so I didn't need to fight in the later rounds. But during my second career in the ring, I learned to use my wisdom more than sheer physical strength. I didn't stand toe-to-toe with another boxer, willing to get my head beat in while I looked for an opportunity to deliver a killer blow that would knock him out. Instead, I learned how to deflect punches so they couldn't hit me. I prepared for the long haul and ran all those miles in training so I could have the energy to last the entire fight. When friends asked me why I was running so much, I told them, "I'm going to lose my knees or my brains. I choose the knees."

Sometimes you need to do something similar in business. You don't always need to be bigger, stronger, or faster. Sometimes you just need to work smarter, to train better, more effectively, or more efficiently. As I said, you don't need to be cutthroat or vicious; instead, look for ways you can improve what you are doing. Focus on one aspect of your career and do that better than anyone else you know.

You might say, "George, you *did* knock out your opponents on your comeback. How can you say you didn't hurt them?"

I learned how to box so I could win the bout without injuring my opponent. If you're not familiar with boxing, a knockout doesn't always mean to be knocked *unconscious*. In most bouts, when a boxer falls to the canvas three times in a round, it counts as a knockout. Sometimes the referee will stop a fight even when a boxer hasn't been knocked down, which counts as a knockout. He's protecting the boxer from being seriously hurt by stopping the fight before it gets to that point.

Earlier in my career, I started building up my rage on Friday to get ready for my match on Saturday. By the time of the fight, I was ready to explode with hatred. When I met my opponent in the middle of the ring to receive the referee's instructions, I would get nose-to-nose and stare him in the eyes. I wanted him to see me fuming, so he would be afraid of me.

But in my second boxing career, I didn't do that. I was the new George, the good George the entire time, from the beginning of my training, all through the match, and even after I climbed out of the ring. I wanted my children to see me on television as a good man—not a mean, hateful guy. I now met all my opponents in the middle of the ring with a big smile on my face.

Ironically, my opponents usually thought I was trying to psyche them out. Sometimes I could hear their trainers yelling at them, "Don't look at him! He's trying to mess with your mind."

Actually I was just being friendly; I wanted to let them know that boxing was a sport to me, and I wasn't angry with them.

The same is true in business. There's plenty of room for all of us. You don't need to drive someone out of business so yours will survive or thrive. Just work hard, strive for excellence, fill a need or provide a benefit, offer good customer service, and keep a smile on your face. You *will* succeed.

BE SLOW TO ANGER

Nor do you need to display anger or spew out a bunch of vile, harsh words to win in business or in your career. I'm not saying you won't ever get mad. The Bible tells us, "A man's discretion makes him slow to anger, and it is his glory to overlook a transgression."[3] Notice that "slow to anger" part. It doesn't say that you will never get angry, but when you do, you are not to lose control of yourself. Don't allow anger to beat you. Sure, there may be times when people around you know that you are really upset, but when you allow something to cause you to lose *self-control*, you are always at a disadvantage.

What should you do when you feel yourself growing angry? If possible, change the subject, or change the activity or the scenery. When you feel anger welling up inside you, take deep breaths, go out for a walk, or punch a punching bag, but don't let the anger overwhelm you to the point that it comes out of your mouth or takes control of your actions, causing you to say or do something foolish. Some people say that it is better to let your anger out than to keep it pent up inside. That may be good advice in psychology class, but it is horrible advice in business. Besides, if you stop *showing* your anger, you might be amazed at how soon you stop *feeling* it.

NEVER CHEAT

You should research the competition and be able to do something that others can't do. Beat the competition fair and square. You don't need to be mean or arrogant, and you certainly should never cheat to win. If you compromise a little to gain a sale or land a promotion, you've lost a lot. Why? You may pocket some money, but you have chipped away a portion of your personal integrity. Besides, if you treat your customers right, they'll keep coming back to do business with you again. But if you are not friendly, helpful, and kind, or if a client detects deceit in you, inevitably you will lose that person's business.

You know how you feel when somebody rips you off. You usually refuse to continue doing business with that person. You'll notice also that word gets around quickly in the business community or in the office regarding someone you should stay away from. So you're always wise to keep your business dealings on the up and up. As a wise businessman said, "You can skin a sheep once, but if you nurture it and take good care of it, you can shear a sheep over and over again."

FOUR WINNING QUALITIES

To make 'em love ya the way I do, you must develop at least four qualities: honesty, enthusiasm, confidence, and courage. Nobody wants to do business with someone he can't trust. That's why you will discover that all truly great businesspeople are honest. Oh sure, you will find some who are not, and for a while they may get ahead. But ultimately their dishonesty will be their undoing. You may be dishonest and get ahead in the short term, but sooner or later your dishonesty will trip you, and you will fall hard and fast. The people with whom you were deceitful will want nothing to do with you.

How much better it is to be honest from the start. Seek to build long-term relationships founded on the truth. If a client, customer, or friend asks you a question and you don't know the answer, don't lie to cover your ignorance. Simply say, "I don't know, but let me check, and I'll get back to you on that." Then do it.

If the price is higher than you know the customer wants to pay, tell him so straightforwardly, and let the customer make the decision. Don't entice the customer with an attractive price and then slip in all sorts of add-ons to boost your profits. Be honest. Tell the customer up front, "Here's what this is going to cost. If you'd like, we can try to save some money on features or eliminate some programs, but for what you want, this is the cost." While you may lose some customers who cannot afford the higher price, you will discover that more people will want to do business with you because they know that you are honorable in your dealings. If you tell them, "This is what it is going to take" and "This is the best deal I can get you," they know they can count on that to be true.

A second key to winning with people is enthusiasm. By enthusiasm I don't mean that you are bombastic or overbearing. An enthusiastic person is excited about life and meets every day as a gift from God. The word *enthused* derives from a word meaning "filled with God." An enthusiastic person is filled with God and is looking forward to seeing what He has in store. Successful people love what they do; their eyes light up when they talk about their work, and their enthusiasm is contagious. Wouldn't you rather be in business with someone who is enthusiastic about her work? When people look at you as a potential partner, employee, or mate, do they see that sort of positive attitude radiating from you?

The third quality that you must develop if you hope to be successful is confidence—a belief in yourself as well as the belief that what you have to offer to somebody else is worthwhile. Confidence is not cockiness; it is a winning attitude. People are attracted to optimism, and if you have an upbeat attitude, they will want you on their teams, they will invite you to their parties or special events, and they will want to introduce you to their friends. On the other hand, when was the last time that you purposely invited a known sourpuss to a party? Your confidence causes other people to feel good when they are around you. Of course, the best kind of confidence is the kind that encourages other people to believe that they can do something great too.

The fourth essential quality is courage. It takes courage to step into a boxing ring, but it takes just as much courage for you to step out of your comfort zone, to attempt to do something significant with your life, to try a new career, to seek a new relationship. Too often, people tend to think, *Oh, what I'm doing isn't that important* or *Maybe other people won't want what I have to offer.* Such thoughts usually spring from a fear of rejection, and it will take real courage to knock on that door of opportunity in front of you. Push past your fears and don't allow anything to keep you from the success you seek. As you make 'em love ya, they will want what you have to offer. A Knockout Entrepreneur never says, "Love it or leave it." A Knockout Entrepreneur says, "I'm gonna make 'em love me so much, they'll never want to go anywhere else."

KNOCKOUT IDEAS
TO STIMULATE YOUR SUCCESS

1. Mr. Ice Cream exhibited two qualities essential for success: enthusiasm and personal integrity. He had a way of making people love him, and

as a result, they were interested in what he had to say and sell. How are these two elements of success evident in your life? Incidentally, if you can't tell, neither can anyone else.

2. Are there some ways in which you act or speak that you intend to portray a particular image, an image of a person who is not the real you? Why not be yourself? Be confident, encouraging, kind, and concerned about others, and you will discover that people love you and want to be involved with you.

3. The Royal Lipizzaner stallions go above and beyond what most horses will do for their owners and trainers. What are you doing that goes beyond the norm or what is necessary to show your appreciation for the people who make your life better?

CHAPTER NINE

KNOW YOUR FOE

A key to success in boxing is knowing your foe. In every field of endeavor, you must deal with the real and also the false perceptions of your competitors. The good news is, if you study your competition, you may be surprised to discover that your opposition isn't nearly as strong as you thought it was.

When I was boxing, people used to tell me all the time, "That Joe Frazier can fight."

"Really?" I said.

"Oh yeah, that Smokin' Joe Frazier can really fight." After a while, I started to believe that Smokin' Joe Frazier could fight.

Years later I was watching some films of Joe's boxing matches and I realized that Joe had only one really effective punch—his left hook. It was a bruising punch, to be sure, but most people walked right into it because they were so afraid that Joe was going to clobber them with his powerful right-hand punches. The films showed me that Joe didn't have a superpowerful right-hand punch. But he and his promoters had put out the word that Joe could really fight. Had I studied films more closely and researched the competition before boxing him, I would have discovered the easy way to beat Joe. I did defeat Smokin' Joe Frazier, but I sure didn't do it the easy way!

Again that willingness to study the competition is a humbling attitude in itself. Every NFL football team studies videotapes of its opponents. But some players have the attitude, "Why do I need to be studying *them*? They should be studying *me*!" The teams that succeed at that high level of play, however, are inevitably the ones that have done their homework. They have studied the competition and learned the weak spots.

When I won the world heavyweight championship the first time, I hardly ever watched films of my competition. I thought I was too good for that. Let them watch films of me! But when I began my quest for a second heavyweight championship, I trained, I hit the road running every day, and I spent hours in front of a punching bag. I also spent hours every day watching films of my competition. When the opportunity came, I was prepared.

Similarly in business, by studying your competitors you can learn what they have and, more important, what they *don't* have. When you learn what your competitors lack, you can make your business more profitable by filling that void and providing that product or service to your competitors' customers as well as your own.

Keep in mind that in boxing, it is not good enough to study the other boxer. You must also study that boxer's coach. You are not trying to overcome just the person in the middle of the ring; you must know the favorite tricks of the trade that his coach has up his sleeve.

In business you may be doing well in competition with those closest to you, but somebody across town may be serving your customers by offering free delivery service. Or perhaps that firm has a Web site that offers special pricing. Whatever it is, you can't simply scout the local competition any more and hope to achieve great success. Get your head out of the sand, lift up your eyes, and see where your customers are going for the lion's share of their needs.

BE ALERT TO UNEXPECTED HELP

During my preparations to fight Evander Holyfield, a friend of mine who was in the gym with Evander while he was working out stopped by to see me regularly. "What's going on over there?" I asked him.

He didn't have anything to do with Holyfield's corner, but he was a conduit of information. Sometimes just a casual, off-the-cuff statement from my friend might give me insight into how I could better train.

When I prepared for a fight, I always tried to outdo my competition. If my competition was spending an hour a day on the punching bag, I'd spend two hours a day punching. Occasionally someone would tell me, "Oh, that guy trains hard!"

If you listen to that sort of talk, you could get nervous and not fight your own fight. So I'd always ask, "Well, what exactly does he do?" Whatever he did, I did more. And I let it be known to the opposition that I was doing more. I wanted him to know that I was prepared. "George, he spends twenty-five minutes in the gym every day." Fine, I'd go into the gym and spend forty-five minutes on each aspect of my training. I'd spend forty-five minutes on the punching bag, another forty-five minutes sparring, and another forty-five minutes on weight training. I'd try to make my opponent's training regimen seem as if he wasn't doing anything. If my opponent ran four miles a day, I'd run six or eight. The good news is that most boxers wanted to run only three or four miles per day. But I have a feeling that several of them wished they had run more after they found out that I had run twice as far.

Don't get angry or envious when people go to your competition instead of you. Find out what your competition is doing, and do more!

Let's say you have a comfortable little business selling donuts and coffee and a major fast-food chain moves in right across the street from you. What are you going to do? Most likely you won't be able to compete with the chain store on its prices, since the chain purchases products and supplies in such large quantities. But you can beat the store by creating an attractive, relaxed environment, having a friendly smile for everyone who comes through your door, and emphasizing personalized customer service. As much as they try, the large chain stores just can't match you on those three elements. Find a service you can provide that the big stores cannot.

Granted, you may lose some business temporarily; people who look only for the least expensive price may not frequent your establishment as often. But people who want a quality product in a comfortable, friendly atmosphere will soon return to find what they can rarely get at the big box stores—somebody who knows their name, and somebody who knows the products. Personally, I will go out of my way to do business where the owners and employers are nice, where they take an interest in me as their customer, and where I receive top-quality, friendly customer service—even if the prices are more expensive.

If you are selling automobiles, the competition is intense and the mark-ups are tight or significantly reduced. You must find an edge that will bring customers back to you long after the initial sale is made. That again usually comes down to service. Provide a clean, friendly atmosphere for your customers, seek to build one-on-one relationships with them, give more than is expected, and you will have a loyal clientele. When I advertised Meineke products, the keys to our success were having a quality product, doing excellent work promptly as advertised, providing a friendly atmosphere, and creating a reputation that "this is a business that can be trusted." Service and trust will beat big and price almost every time.

PERCEPTION IS REALITY—WHAT
THEY SEE IS WHAT YOU GET!

Regardless of what you are experiencing, whether you are doing well or poorly, try to put on the best face possible because your customers, clients, friends, and family will take their cues from you. By maintaining a strong posture, you will win the support of those around you, which will boost your confidence while draining that of your opposition. In boxing, unless a fighter is staggering around, gasping for air, or lying on the floor, the opposition's perception of your condition becomes his reality. In your situation, the picture you present to your competition and to the public is what the competition and public see. No one will know that you have a broken hand or a cracked rib unless you reveal it. Often the worst thing you can do is to let your competition know where and how you are hurting. Why? Because that is precisely where they will hit you. Furthermore, if the public senses that you are on a downward trend, your chances of enlisting the public's support become minimal.

Regardless of your feelings, ailments, concerns, or doubts, you must commit to a confident, capable appearance. Your positive, upbeat demeanor may cause your opponents to change their strategy or to abandon certain tactics on which they have been working. They may assume that those tactics are proving ineffective, and they may be tempted to do some things they might not ordinarily do, something in which they have little expertise, or something they have not previously done or practiced in training camp. This can easily work to your favor.

Additionally, your confident appearance, even when things are not going well, will prevent your opposition from gaining undue hope that you are going down for the count. They may think that if they increase their intensity and pummel your weaknesses, you will eventually give up, crumble, and cave.

That's one reason during my comeback career that I always stood in my corner between rounds rather than sit down as was permitted, and as most of my opponents did. I wanted to convey an image to my competition that I was still strong and ready to battle. Besides, when I was in training, I never sat down, so I didn't want to sit down during an actual match. I'd come over to my corner and sometimes I'd even try to cheer up my cornermen. "Hey, guys, how are we doin'?" I'd prompt them.

"Oh, we're doing great, George! Keep up the good work."

I'd turn around and face my opponent as he looked over at us, a happy bunch of guys, and I could almost see the wheels turning in his head as he started trying to find ways he could quit! Truth is, it sometimes doesn't affect the other fighter as much as it does the men in his corner. "Oh, watch out; we better play it safe," they might whisper among themselves. "George is getting even stronger in these last rounds."

Maintaining a confident appearance involves everything from the way you hold yourself, your overall demeanor, to the way you dress, to the way you take care of the car you drive, to the expressions on your face, to the words that come out of your mouth. The old saying "Money attracts money" has merit. If you give the appearance that you are confident, competent, and successful, people will assume that you are and will be more likely to want to do business with you, to have you as part of their organization, or to hire you.

On the other hand, if you look like a ragtag operation, someone who may not be with the firm next month or whose business is headed toward bankruptcy, few people will want to take a chance on you. Certainly you should not be pretentious about your external appearances. There's no need to wear more expensive clothing than you can afford or live in a home you cannot afford simply to make an impression. But use what resources you have wisely and present the best image possible to your clients as well as your competitors. Their perception of you becomes their reality. That's why you should keep a smile on your face, no matter what trouble you are going through.

Once I was having disagreements with my producers during the filming of one of my television programs. The tension was taking a toll on me and affecting my performance. A good friend gave me a piece of advice: "George, no matter what problems you have with some of the people you are working with, when you are on screen, nobody sees that. Nobody knows. Do. your job on screen, and deal with the other problems off the air." That was wise counsel because the people who were tuning in to watch our show were looking for good quality, funny, uplifting entertainment. Anything that interfered with me providing that "product" had to be put off until later.

When I first started promoting my boxing comeback and I appeared on television, I was determined to keep it light, to have fun with the interviewer and never get too serious for long. People didn't want to hear about my problems; they had enough troubles of their own. They weren't tuning in to a late-night talk show to be depressed; they wanted to be entertained. So anytime an interview started to get too serious, I'd try to make a joke of something, usually in a self-deprecating manner.

About that same time, the young boxing phenomenon Mike Tyson was talking tough, saying in interviews how he was going to crack somebody's nose.

"Yeah, but I'm going to hide!" I quipped.

"But, George, you're too old to be boxing."

"Well, yes, but when I was younger, I had my left and my right," I'd say as I swiped fake punches in the interviewer's direction with my left and right fists. "But now, if I miss you with my left or right, look! I've got a belly bump!" I pushed my belly out like Santa Claus, and the audience roared in laughter.

Sure, I had problems, and yes, I desperately needed people to come out to the fights. Frankly, I needed the money for my family and me to survive, and later on, for the George Foreman Youth and Community Center to survive. But I never took my problems public. I knew that everybody tuning in was already carrying a heavy load; I didn't want to do anything to increase the burdens of the audience. Instead I hoped to lift their spirits a bit. Even in our church, I never took my problems to the pulpit.

There's something to be said for looking successful even when you are not. But there's something even more impressive about showing how happy and content you are. A lot of people who appear to be successful are up to their eyeballs in debt, wondering how they are going to make the next payment on their fancy cars or luxurious homes. Better than merely looking the part, develop a confident upbeat attitude, and you will be amazed how truly successful people are attracted to you. People want to be around somebody who is positive, encouraging, and uplifting. Beyond that, employers want to employ and promote people who are pleasant and see the best in others. If you are in business, maintain an upbeat attitude, and if for some reason you find that you cannot, either find a new line of work or find people who do have a positive upbeat attitude to represent you well to your customers.

A frequently overlooked significant member of your team is your receptionist. The person who greets guests with a smile and a friendly "Hello, welcome!" or the person who answers your telephone is the most important person in your company. Why? Because that person presents the first impression of who you are and the type of company you are. By the tone of voice, that person either welcomes people or implies that you could care less about the call. Make sure your receptionist knows the valuable impact the person in that position can make. Encourage your receptionist to smile when answering the phone. The smile will come out in her voice and make a better impression on your callers.

In the same way, every time you are on the telephone, smile. Believe it or not you will come across more friendly as you speak, and that will improve the impression you are making.

Another place where you can sometimes make a good impression and get a notch up on the competition is the staff meeting. Because these meetings occur often and are usually rather informal, people who are not cued in to success frequently step into these meetings unprepared. That is a big mistake. Your poor preparation is a loud statement about yourself, even if you don't open your mouth during the meeting. Then again, maybe you are reluctant to speak up during the meeting because you know you are unprepared. What a wasted opportunity. Gathered in that staff meeting may be your peers and at least one of your superiors. They will draw many of their conclusions about your competence, creativity, and value to the team based on your performance in those meetings. Why miss a golden opportunity to set yourself apart from the crowd? Be careful to present yourself as knowledgeable but not a know-it-all. Don't put anyone else down or try to butter up the boss. Simply do your homework and attend all staff meetings prepared to discuss the issues at hand and to make suggestions, whether you are a main presenter or not. By looking and sounding prepared, you will establish yourself as a person headed for success.

FINISH THE JOB FIRST

A key principle in boxing is this: when your competition is hurt or has been knocked down, don't give him the opportunity to recover. There will be plenty of time for kindness and altruism later, but when you find an advantage, you must capitalize on it while you can.

A good boxer will get back up and fight even harder after having been knocked down, maybe even harder than you, making the match much more difficult to win. That's why you must seize the moment when you have your competitor off balance and do everything you can do to take the "fight" out of him or take him out of the fight. Do all you can to maintain the upper hand.

If your competition gets knocked down and stays down, you can be the first to help him back up when the fight is over. Oftentimes you can convince your former opponents to join your team. Allies recruited in defeat will prove to be most spirited in battle as they seek both success and redemption. You may also learn a great deal from them about other competitors.

Angelo Dundee and Gil Clancy were key members of my team whom I recruited from other competitors. Both became integral parts of my success. Had they not been strong competitors once trying to beat me, I might not have had the enormous respect for them that I had.

But in the midst of the fight, you have to stay focused on getting the job done. Once I was in a boxing match in Las Vegas and I knew I had my opponent on the run, but he wouldn't quit and he wouldn't fall. I respected him for that, but I sure didn't want to injure the man. I kept hitting him with strong right-hand punches, causing him to reel and turn, yet he stayed on his feet. Seeing that my opponent was hurting, I attempted to be benevolent. I said, "Hey, ref, the guy can't take any more."

The referee waved me off, so I hit my opponent a couple more times. It was plain to me that the guy was out of it, so I eased up on him. "Whatcha gonna do, ref?" I asked when the bell rang, ending the round. The referee did nothing.

But in the next round, my opponent seemed to have gotten a fresh wind. He received my gift of mercy and reciprocated with a gift of power. He came roaring back at me with incredible strength, pounding on my body. By the time the fight was over, I looked like the cowardly lion, all puffy and swollen. I won the fight, but I learned a valuable lesson: finish the job first, then extend kindness to the opponent. After I had earned the right to be heard, I could say good things about my competition, but not in the heat of the battle.

In the same way, you need to be aggressive about your career. You don't need to trample people in your way. Remember the old adage "Be nice to the people on your way up because you will meet them again on your way down"—but stay focused on where you are going and how you plan to get there.

BE MORE ACCESSIBLE

Another reason to study your competition is to be more accessible than your competitors. Give your customers something with which they can identify, something that establishes a relationship with them. Before I started promoting the George Foreman Lean, Mean, Fat-Reducing Grilling Machine, I knew about Weber Grills, our main competitor. They made a fine product and were quite successful. I ate at their restaurant anytime I was in the Chicago area. They were a great company and had great products, but they were just a company. Their products were "untouchable." That is, there was nobody with whom the public could identify; they didn't have a company spokesperson, logo, or image that stuck in the minds of people; they didn't relate to people and seemed removed from their customers. So when we began promoting the George Foreman grill, I wanted it to be a product people could touch, with an image they could relate to, as they associated the grill with me. That's why we put my smiling picture on the packaging, and that's why I appeared on late-night talk shows and infomercials—so people could associate the product with me.

When they walked through their local department store and saw the grill, they'd see a picture of me smiling on the package and immediately make that association. Oftentimes people bought the product because they connected it to the advertising they had seen. They didn't even know for sure that it worked. Of course, once they tried the product, they loved it, but that initial association was with a person—not a product.

You'll find the same is true in your business and career. Customers, coworkers, or clients will "buy" you long before they buy what you have to say or sell. That's why your first impression is so important. You are making an emotional connection with that other person, who is consciously or sub-consciously deciding whether or not to do business with you. Be friendly and accessible; let people know that you are excited about what you are doing, and hopefully they will remember that the next time they are looking for someone who can do what you do.

Why do NASCAR racing teams and Indy car racing teams cover their cars and uniforms with company logos as advertisements? The cars would run just as well without the fancy paint jobs. The fire suits would be just as effective if they were a plain vanilla white or all black. But the team owners know that people identify their "product" by those logos, and identifying the logos with the driver or race team boosts awareness. Those logos involve megabucks deals nowadays, but even more important than that, the logos make the product or service touchable. The logos make the team identifiable to the consumer.

STAY WITH THE PEOPLE

I often hear celebrities talking about how they don't dare mingle with the crowds because there are so many autograph hounds and paparazzi tagging along everywhere they go. I understand what they mean, but I think they are missing a lot of good opportunities. Funny, isn't it? People will do almost anything to become famous, and then when they make it, they don't want to do the very things that helped them become successful in the first place.

Some business executives, politicians, and others refuse to fly commercially anymore and demand private aircraft. They spend exorbitant amounts of money to avoid the very people they need to be brushing shoulders with if they hope to keep in touch with everyday needs. I used to fly private aircraft, and granted, it is convenient. After a while, though, it becomes an excuse to avoid the public. I decided that I was losing touch with people by flying privately. I fly commercially these days, and I learned quickly that although there are a few pests, most people are pretty nice.

One time I was at the lake, and I wanted to fish, but I'd heard that there were a lot of snakes in the lake. A friend of mine told me, "George, I go out every spring to clear the snakes out of the lake. And I found out, there really aren't that many snakes; it just seems like there are a lot when you see one or two."

He was right, not merely about the snakes in the lake, but about people too. Most people want to be friendly; they are not vicious. They don't bite. Sure, you may meet a mean one every now and then, but as a rule most people try to be nice. Most people are looking for the same thing you are—a good, peaceful, happy life.

Sometimes I'll go to the grocery store in the evening, and inevitably somebody will see me and call out, "George! George Foreman!" I always try to take the time to say hello and to sign an autograph. Sometimes a crowd will gather, but in most cases I'll just be friendly and be on my way. Occasionally, I'll get stuck signing autographs for a half hour or so, but I don't usually mind—unless I've been shopping for ice cream! I look at that time as an investment. I'm establishing a personal relationship by being accessible, and many of those people become customers for some of my products. It all begins by establishing a good relationship.

Losing contact with people is much more dangerous to your business and your personal success. You can become untouchable and, more important, *untouched* by the people around you.

SERVE AND SUCCEED

Probably as much as anyone in the past forty years, Sam Walton, founder of Wal-Mart, understood the necessity of studying the competition, looking for trends, and serving his customers. In 1971, seven years after Wal-Mart was born, Sam wrote to all of his associates (employees):

> If any generalization is true of retailing in the 70s, it would have to be that our business is one of constant change. Increasingly, this is just as true in our small trade centers as well as in the larger metropolitan areas. Consequently it is most important that all of us in Wal-Mart be alert and curious to new trends and developments in retailing. It is imperative that each new process be studied and analyzed thoroughly to see if we can adopt the idea for Wal-Mart, but the total key for our stores is that we retain our philosophy of being not only the dominant store in our areas, but more importantly, that we do the best job of anybody around in rendering effective, friendly customer service.[1]

No wonder that by 2005 Sam Walton's stores could be found in nearly five thousand US locations and earning more than $257 billion in sales!

If you really want to be a success in life and feel as though your life has significance, if you want to be happy in your family or career relationships and win big in business, then learn how to serve well. Recognize that any legitimate, good quality work is never demeaning, but is always noble if done well. It is usually quite profitable as well.

In New York's JFK International Airport, there is a shoeshine stand where the man who cleans and shines other people's shoes regards his work as a noble calling and always does it with excellence. Some people will walk a half-mile or more across the huge airport concourse just to have that particular shoeshine man work on their shoes. He's that good. He makes every customer feel special, offers astute observations on the travelers passing by, and engages every person who sits in his stand in uplifting conversation.

Not surprisingly, the man at that shoe-shine station is not someone who couldn't get a job anywhere else or doesn't have any skills beyond cleaning and polishing shoes. In fact, he owns fourteen shoeshine operations in New York, operated mostly by members of his immediate family and other relatives. He doesn't need to shine shoes for a living—he simply loves people and loves his work. He sees shining shoes as a service he can provide, something he can do well, maybe better than most. In the process he has become wonderfully wealthy.

I remember another elderly gentleman who had a shoeshine business in Burbank, California, right in the NBC television studio complex, near the *Tonight Show* studios. At that time Johnny Carson was the host of the show, and every time Johnny asked me to come on the program, I stopped at the man's shoeshine chair on the way. He would shine my shoes and then bring them back to the dressing room. Above his chair on the walls, he had signed photographs from such major entertainers as Bob Hope, Sammy Davis Jr., and Jack Benny.

When the shoeshine man decided to retire, Johnny Carson had him come on national television. Johnny said, "Tonight we have a special treat. We have the best shoeshine man in the world." He went on to introduce the shoeshine man and told how he had been working at NBC for all those years. I've never forgotten that image of the shoeshine man sitting on the *Tonight Show* dais with Johnny Carson. The lesson was clear to me: do the best you can, and you will be remembered, even if your business is shining shoes. If you do it with an attitude to serve, your gift will make a way for you; your talent will take you places other people will never get to see.

Many people think serving others means servitude. Nothing could be further from the truth. Serving is giving the other person what he or she needs to function in the best way possible. In the Old Testament the same word is used to describe serving God and serving each other. Interesting, isn't it? Only human beings can do both by choice—worship God and serve our fellow man. In fact, you might say this is one of the key distinctions between man and beasts. No animal ever willingly serves another; only human beings can choose to serve other human beings.

Another person who learned this lesson well is George Zimmer. You may not recognize his name, but you have probably seen George on television advertising his clothing stores. Like a lot of men, George never really enjoyed shopping for his clothes, especially clothes he could wear to work. He got to thinking about that and talking with a few other fellows, and he quickly surmised that he was not alone in his distaste for trolling through the menswear section in the department stores. In 1973, George Zimmer opened a clothing store in Houston that he called Men's Wearhouse. The store reflected George's conviction that "the average man enjoys shopping for clothes about as much as going to the dentist."

So George sought to make it easy for men to find clothes that they could wear (and that their wives would approve of them wearing), at prices they didn't mind paying. Like most successful entrepreneurs, he discovered a need and found a way to fill it. George enlisted a sales force and taught them how to serve the customers, and how to feel excited about it. Today, Men's Wearhouse has more than six thousand employees in about four hundred stores across the nation. George's service-oriented men's stores are now worth more than one billion dollars! In 2009, *Fortune* magazine named Men's Wearhouse as one of the 100 Best Companies to Work for in America. You've probably heard one of George's most famous slogans: "You're gonna love the way you look. I guarantee it!"

Jesus said that He came not to be served, but to serve. Instead of worrying about who gets the biggest piece of the pie, try serving the pie to others! Make the pie bigger so more people can enjoy success. An interesting phenomenon takes place when you consistently serve other people—you will often discover that when you need help the most, other people will be there for you. In business, if you take care of your customers, they will take care of you. Give other people an opportunity to succeed and they will help you succeed. As Zig Ziglar, the world-famous motivational speaker and author, puts it, "You can get everything in life you want, if you help enough other people get what they want."[2]

But you must be sincere. Trying to give people what they want so you can get what you want will not work well for you in the long run. People can smell insincerity. If they think for a moment that you have ulterior motives and you aren't really concerned about their needs or their success, they will shy away from you and your product or services.

On the other hand, if you build your business by building solid relationships with clients, attempting to serve them with no thought of immediate reward or personal return, rewards will come your way, and your customers will return time after time. Just make sure your friends, clients, or customers know that you are there to help them. To put it bluntly: make yourself needed. Better yet, make yourself indispensable. You can do that by knowing more about your area of expertise than others or by providing an exclusive service that you do better than anyone else. The best-paid people in the world have found a way to make themselves needed.

It is not hard work alone that will make you indispensable. Lots of people work hard. People who scrub the floors in fast-food restaurants work hard and gravediggers work hard, but neither group will ever be highly paid for their hard work. The people who command today's top salaries are usually individuals who work hard with creativity and innovation, have good judgment, and are problem solvers willing to go the extra mile for their clients.

Granted, business exists to meet needs, and successful businesses do a better job of meeting their customers' needs for a particular product or service. But remember, your company's greatest need is not for new product lines; its primary need is for competent, creative people who are willing and able to serve other people.

DON'T WORRY ABOUT WHO GETS THE CREDIT

Rather than think about who gets the credit, focus your concern on doing the job the best way for all concerned. When I was making my comeback in boxing, I attempted to secure my boxing license in Los Angeles, one of the most difficult places in America to get a boxing license. I figured that if I could pass the rigorous tests there, I'd have it made getting licenses to fight in other states.

The process was intense, though. The doctors in LA didn't really want to grant me a license because they feared I was too old to box. My doctor developed a number of tests to show that I was healthy and able to compete. All of my tests came out perfectly.

The California attorney general was also on the boxing board, and he was worried that I might bring a suit against the state if I got hurt. "George, why do you want to box?" he asked.

"Life, liberty, and the pursuit of *my* happiness," I replied without hesitation.

Another attorney said, "Look, this guy has satisfied every requirement and done far more diagnostic tests than necessary. I suggest we give him a license."

Eventually, after I satisfied the state's many demands, California granted me a license and I went on to win the world heavyweight boxing championship for the second time in my life, at forty-five years of age—older than any man ever to win the crown.

Later I wrote the book *By George*, describing my rise to fame and fortune. The NBC television network was interested in developing the story line into a made-for-television movie. My friend and agent at that time, Jeff Wall, worked on the deal, and as we were working on the screenplay, we got together with my good friend Sylvester Stallone. Jeff showed Stallone some of our ideas and asked, "What do you think, Sly? Do you think this story line will work?"

Stallone loved the ideas so much, he incorporated them into a movie of his own a number of years later, *Rocky Balboa*. When Jeff saw the script for the Stallone movie, Jeff brought it to me. "George, look at this."

As I read the script, I realized that much of the plot in my friend's movie was loosely based on my life and experiences during my comeback. Ironically, NBC television never produced the movie based on my book *By George*, but Stallone kept elements of the story and took it to the entire world.

Was I angry that Sly Stallone used elements of my story in his? No way! It is not important who gets the credit as long as something good gets done.

I'm delighted and honored that Sylvester Stallone could draw from my experience and make something that entertained and perhaps inspired many other people. It was a high compliment. Besides, my story doesn't simply belong to me; it is a story for the world, all for the glory of God.

A Knockout Entrepreneur knows that studying the competition will provide tremendous insights into what you can do better—how you can better serve your clients, how you can provide something that your competitors cannot. But if you focus only on the competition, you will always be in a defensive mode. Instead, constantly be on the lookout for fresh ways to do what you do; stay alert for new ideas to expand your market or to make your product or service more effective. As you do you will encounter one of the most daunting and formidable foes you will ever face—*change*! But Knockout Entrepreneurs aren't afraid of change; in fact, they welcome it, as we'll see in the next chapter.

KNOCKOUT IDEAS
TO STIMULATE YOUR SUCCESS

1. Identify your main competitors in business or your career. What are they doing better than you? What are they leaving undone? What can you do to improve your efforts in those areas?

2. What are the most obvious obstacles blocking your personal success?

3. What steps can you begin taking today to overcome those obstacles?

4. List two things you can do this month to show your competitors and yourself that you are interested in their success. Be specific. What will it require for you to do those two things, and when will you begin?

CHAPTER TEN

THE TOUGHEST STEP TO SUCCESS

S ir Edmund Hillary climbed Mount Everest in 1953. What made that such an incredible feat? It had never been done before. Every year since then, dozens of mountain climbers have successfully scaled Mount Everest. Why is it easier to climb Mount Everest now? And why do we make such a big deal about Sir Edmund Hillary being the first to climb that mountain? Simple. When Hillary set out on the climb, he didn't know for sure that it could be done. He especially didn't know that *he* could do it. A challenge isn't nearly so ominous when you know it can be done, but it takes great risk and great faith to attempt something that has never been done before.

The world is full of people who want to play it safe, people who have tremendous potential but never use it. Somewhere deep inside them, they know that they could do more in life, be more, and have more—if only they were willing to take a few risks.

Taking risks, trying something new, developing new ideas for products and services that meet emerging needs in the future—that's what being a Knockout Entrepreneur is all about. For example, the struggling entrepreneur who invented plastic gift cards is now a multimillionaire. He convinced a few stores that rather than offer credit cards, they should offer gift cards that the public could purchase in places other than the store whose name was on the card. "Why would we want our gift cards in somebody else's store?" he heard again and again.

"Because people shop there for other things, and they have only limited time for shopping. They will see your gift cards as a convenience and will appreciate you saving them time and another stop," he replied.

He had an uphill battle getting the marketing teams to change their fundamental method of doing business. But after a few failed attempts, the gift card business caught on. Now you can purchase everything from restaurant gift cards to auto service cards, right at your grocery store!

Changing the fundamentals isn't easy, and to do so, you mustn't be afraid to buck the status quo. When I was making my comeback, I found that I couldn't hit as well with my right hand as I had in the past, so I worked twice as much on using my left hand. Normally, a boxer will go in tight circles to the left as he moves around the ring, but during my comeback, I practiced moving to the right. Boxers who watched me on film moving to the left were caught off guard when I came out and moved so effectively to the right. I'm convinced that by being willing to make that fundamental change, I gave myself an advantage that took me all the way to the top. But I had to be willing to change.

Don't be afraid to change your strategy, switch your footing, or adapt on the fly. Always keep a little something that you can fall back on. In a fight I nearly lost, I changed my footing, adapted my stance, and won. You may have to do something similar with your business at times. There's no shame in changing—especially when what you are doing isn't working well—just have a good reason for making the change.

Get in the habit of asking yourself probing questions, such as: *How can I do what I do better than I am currently doing it? How can I better develop my creative skills? Am I problem oriented or solution oriented? Are there changes that I need to consider?*

Our resistance to change usually involves fear of the unknown coupled with a desire to maintain the status quo. Many people are more comfortable with what they already know and would rather remain where they are than risk stepping out into the unknown. That is a normal reaction, but successful people regularly overcome this resistance. They realize that most fears about change are groundless. Or maybe they have decided that the fear of the unknown is far less than the torture and tedium of spending the rest of their lives tied to a job, career, relationship, or lifestyle that they find unrewarding, demeaning, boring, and insignificant. In that case, change—as disconcerting as it may be—is the far better alternative.

ALWAYS BE READY TO ADJUST TO THE ELEMENTS

Sometimes you have to be flexible and willing to adjust or adapt to changing conditions. As the old saying reminds us, "You can plan a pretty picnic, but you can't predict the weather." Certainly you should always plan, and you should plan to follow your plan. But when the unexpected happens or you discover that your plan just isn't working very well, you must be willing to carefully adjust your approach. If you don't, you risk defeat, embarrassment, or worse.

In a boxing match you can control many things, but there are some things, just like the weather, that can vary in your favor or in your opponent's favor. Always have a contingency plan, and be prepared to use it.

LEARN TO PLAY POSSUM

Have you ever seen a real, live possum? Truth is, a live possum often looks about the same as a dead one, and that is one of his best defenses—appearing weak and helpless when he is strong and vital. Sometimes in business you need to appear weak when in reality you are moving toward your goal.

When I came back to boxing, I wanted to wear a pair of old red trunks that I had worn during my first quest for the championship. You may wonder, "What difference does it make, George, about the color of trunks you wear when you are boxing?" None at all, really, but I had won a lot of boxing matches wearing those red trunks, and I had an almost sentimental feeling about them. When I first started back, I learned that I couldn't wear that color since my opponent had already chosen red.

"You'll have to wear the white trunks, George," the promoter said.

I went to Archie Moore, my cornerman at the time. "Archie, they're taking away my red trunks," I complained.

Archie rubbed his chin and nonchalantly said, "You don't need them anyway. They'll be the first thing you take off after the fight."

He was trying to impress upon me that the change shouldn't shake me. People are always looking for ways to shake you up. If you allow them to get away with it, you have given them the upper hand. I decided then and there that it didn't matter what color of trunks I wore. I was going to win, and my victory would not be based on some superstition or good luck charm. It would be based on hard work, discipline, and the goodness of God. Your success should be based on those same things.

I finally got to where I could play a pretty good possum, though. For instance, in a boxing match both fighters must wear the same type of glove, which is negotiated long before the fight. I preferred wearing a smaller, Reyes brand of boxing glove, known as a puncher's glove. The other glove of choice was the Everlast glove, which seemed to have a little more cushion—although I had been knocked out by the Everlast glove too.

Before I fought Michael Moorer for the championship, we got together in the prefight meetings and Michael said that he wanted to use the Reyes gloves for our fight.

"The *Reyes* glove?" I pretended to balk and gave Michael a stern look of consternation.

"Yeah, that's right. We're going to use the Reyes glove," Michael said. "That can't be changed."

"Oh no!" I feigned. "Well, okay, if that's the way you want it—"

"Yes, that's the way I want it."

I almost shouted, "Glory, hallelujah!" on the way out of that meeting. But of course, I didn't let Michael's team know that the Reyes glove was the one I really wanted to use. In fact, I didn't say another word about it until after the fight when I was the new heavyweight champion of the world.

Learn to play possum a little. Don't let others know when you are hurt or when you are upset or angry about something. Instead, let them think that they have gotten something over on you, and you can turn that possumlike weakness into a strength.

I did something similar when I was negotiating with fight promoter Bob Arum for one of my first fights in Las Vegas during my comeback. Nobody wanted to promote a fight near Christmastime, but I needed to fight. I was trying to stay in shape, plus I really did need the money.

I finally talked Bob Arum into promoting a Vegas fight a week or two before Christmas. Bob knew I was desperate. "Okay, I'll do it, but I'm only going to do one boxing match," he groused. "I'm not going to do a series of three fights."

"Okay, great," I said. I wanted to sign on for only one fight anyhow.

"Well, I can only pay you twelve thousand five hundred dollars," Bob said firmly.

"Okay," I said in my best possum's voice. I only needed $12,500. Besides that, I knew that Bob had to feel that he was winning with that price. If he was, he wouldn't come down in the future; he'd only go up. Once he said a certain price, he wouldn't move; he would try to win, to close the deal with that price. So I played possum and agreed to that price. Bob was pleasantly surprised that I didn't try to get more money out of him.

The response and the ratings were so good on the initial Las Vegas fight, it wasn't long before Bob came back to me and said, "I want to put on another fight with you."

"Okay," I responded.

"But I can only pay you twenty-five thousand dollars."

"Okay, great!" I responded. I knew that Bob wouldn't come down. He was thinking he had me for a bargain barrel price, but I was playing possum, knowing that if I could keep winning, Bob would keep running up the price.

The next fight, Bob was willing to pay me $100,000.

Great! Bob was feeling that he was beating me in the negotiations, and of course, I was glad to let him win because I was making more money with each match. The next fight, he came in at one million dollars! I won the next two fights for one million dollars each. Then it came time for the bout with Evander Holyfield. It was a *big* deal.

Bob came into the room and heaved a big sigh. "Well, George, we got the fight. But we can only pay you twelve and a half million—"

Ha! I had started at $12,500! Now Bob was paying me a fortune. Remember, I was just as content with the $12,500 as I was the $12.5 million!

But believe me, I cashed the check! I made Bob a lot of money too, but what he perceived as a weakness, I knew was a strength.

No matter the size of the deals you are doing, the principle remains the same: sometimes you have to play a little possum, to lie low, pretending that you aren't all that interested when, in time, you know that it will be a winning situation for both you and the person with whom you are working.

WHEN TIMES ARE TOUGH, KEEP LOOKING UP

When times are difficult, maintain your integrity and do your best to give other people some extra grace. Understand that they might be nervous, that they may be going through tough times as well; that they might be worried because of difficult circumstances or their bad decisions. Often in the midst of stressful situations, new entrepreneurial ventures are considered and new businesses are birthed.

Rather than look at life through the lens of problems and obstacles, consider temporary setbacks as opportunities and challenges. That's what a young lady named Paula had to do. When Paula graduated from high school, she married her high school sweetheart and set out to conquer the world, assuming she'd be the perfect wife and mom, and he'd be the best husband and dad. Before long, though, life took some nasty turns. Paula's father died unexpectedly, followed by the heartbreaking loss of her mother a few years later, when Paula was only twenty-three years of age and had two little boys of her own to care for.

All of Paula's props of security were swept out from under her. By the time Paula was forty, her husband was gone and she was experiencing regular panic attacks, so severe that she was afraid to leave her home. Finally Paula decided that she couldn't depend on other people to make her happy anymore. She took control of her life and with only two hundred dollars, she and her sons began a fledgling food service company using her grandmother's recipes. Paula made the food, and the boys and she delivered bag lunches to offices and stores in town. She whimsically called her company "The Bag Lady."

She provided an excellent product with prompt delivery, so her business soon grew from a lunch and catering service to a full-service restaurant. She and her sons leased a building downtown and opened for business, still using some of Grandma's favorite recipes.

Today, Paula Deen is the queen of southern cooking. Her upbeat, vivacious personality and her obvious love for what she does have propelled her restaurants and cookbooks to enormous success. She has her own magazine and her own television series, all because she refused to give up and refused to be dominated by difficult circumstances, heartache, or suffering. Instead, she has kept her attitude on the positive side of life, and she continues to enjoy enormous success.

AVOID EMPHASIZING THE NEGATIVE

When the George Foreman grill first came out, some marketing people suggested that we try to promote our product by showing how unsafe charcoal and gas grills were in comparison to our electric grill. They had pictures and videotapes of fires that had been caused by charcoal and gas grills. I felt that was focusing on the negative.

I said, "That isn't going to happen. If our product is better, let's show people that. I don't want to build our business by talking badly about someone else."

We called a big meeting to discuss the matter, and the marketers said, "You don't have to do it, George. We'll do it."

"I'm not going to do the deal then," I said. I emphatically repeated my position. "I'm not going to knock someone's product to prove how good ours is. If our product is so good, let's show the public how good it is."

The marketers went back to the drawing board and had all sorts of meetings. They finally came out with a marketing plan that showed how great the George Foreman grill performed without putting down other people's products. I went on television in an infomercial format promoting the positive qualities of the grill, and people bought it. They've been buying George Foreman grills ever since!

KEEP YOUR PLAN FLEXIBLE

Although goal setting is important for any successful business, don't allow yourself or your employees to become a slave to schedules, flow charts, quotas, or other man-made, arbitrary structures. When an opportunity or human need comes up, be quick to shift gears, change directions, and allow yourself the freedom and flexibility to do something spontaneous. Recognizing a need and taking timely steps to meet it will lead to success more often than the best-intentioned business plan or focus groups.

How can you ever win if you never take a risk? The truth is, all of life is a risk. Getting out of bed each morning is a risk; getting married is a risk; having a baby is a colossal risk! Starting a business is risky, and when you take a risk, you always have the possibility of losing. But if you never take a risk, you forfeit the chance to succeed.

All highly successful people seem to have a high willingness to take a risk. That doesn't mean they are foolish or reckless; far from it. In fact, some of the biggest risk takers are often extremely thoughtful and disciplined people. But when opportunity came their way, they were willing to take a chance. They were willing to count the costs and then take calculated risks to accomplish their goals.

Most successful risk takers consider best-case and worst-case scenarios before taking a leap of faith into the darkness. But they refuse to be stuck in a rut of indecision. Peter Drucker put it well: "You can count on it: wherever you see a successful business, someone once made a courageous decision."[1] Of course, the better decisions you make, the more likely your success will be.

To make better decisions, gather as much of the best information as you can, but don't procrastinate making a decision based on not enough information. You rarely have *enough* information to make a risky decision; if the information was that readily available, there would be limited risk. But sooner or later, you must decide that you have enough information to make an intelligent, confident decision based on what you know. Make a list of pros and cons—the old-fashioned practice of listing them on opposite sides of a ledger still provides great insight. Listen to competent advisors, but don't ignore your instincts and intuition. Sometimes you just have to "trust your gut" and go for it!

Sure, you may go through tough times when you first risk making a change, but if you approach the change with courage and the determination to willfully and voluntarily choose a new direction, you will come through the tough times with flying colors, and you will be much stronger as a result.

One of the worst things I can think of would be to reach the end of my life, asking myself the following questions: *Why didn't I take that opportunity to do something different? Why didn't I risk doing what I really wanted to do in life? Why did I allow myself to be sidetracked into a mediocre career that I didn't care about? Why didn't I at least try to change?*

Don't let that happen to you. Start making the changes today that will make the remainder of your life happier, more fulfilling, and more significant.

YOU GOTTA BE WILLING TO CHANGE

Change makes most people uncomfortable at first. We shouldn't be surprised at that since we grow accustomed to the way we do things, and for the most part we do what we really want to do in the way that we want to do it. So when our world gets dashed by change, it is easy to become disconcerted. I don't think it is wise to embrace every desire for change just on the basis that it is different. But change can be good, especially when it comes to looking for ways to do things better than I am doing them currently.

If you spend most of your time with people who are entrenched in "the way we do things around here" or "this is how we've always done it," you'll soon take on those worn-out ideas and unbending attitudes. But if you keep people with a willingness to change on your team, you'll find that they are always coming up with something new and exciting. Not only that, but they will inspire you to dig deeper and do more, to get more out of yourself than you thought possible.

About the time I was preparing to get back into boxing, I saw an interview on ESPN with Chicago Bears linebacker Mike Singletary, one of the greatest football players to ever hold his position. What struck me about the interview was that they were talking as though Mike was really old, almost as if his career was over. To me, he was just a kid!

Mike admitted that when he was a relative newcomer to the NFL, he found himself wearing down too early in the game. By the end of the game, he was running on empty. He asked a fitness coach what he could do to improve his endurance, and the trainer suggested riding a stationary bike. "Get on that bike and give me ten miles," the trainer told him.

Mike mounted the stationary bike and worked it like crazy. *Pssszzzzz!* The pedals flew around. After about twenty minutes, Mike began to slow down. "Hey!" the trainer called out to him. "When are you going to give me those ten miles?"

Mike went back to work, pedaling the ten miles. When he finished, he told the coach, "I did it!"

"I knew you could," the fitness coach said with a smile.

When I heard that interview, I got inspired. I decided to run ten miles a day in my training. Keep in mind, I hadn't run ten blocks in more than ten years! When I first started out, I tired quickly, but each day I tried to go a little farther. I remembered that Mike Singletary interview, and I slowed down a bit, then gave it another shot. Little by little, I increased my endurance to the point I could run ten miles. I realized that a young person had inspired me.

I watched another interview, this time with Mike Tyson when he first came into boxing prominence. During the interview, Mike confessed that he didn't punch a hard leather punching bag anymore. I was surprised, but intrigued. Mike said that he hit the leather bag so hard that his knuckles and hands would swell and sometimes even break open in cuts. He said that he found out he could get just as good a workout by punching a water-filled punching bag, and it didn't cause his hands to swell.

Mmmm, maybe that youngster has something there, I thought.

I tried Mike's idea of training with a water-filled punching bag, and I discovered that he was right. It didn't bother my hands nearly as much, and I was still getting a good workout. I had to laugh as I went through my training routines each day and realized that those youngsters had helped this older fellow prepare to regain the world heavyweight title!

In a similar way, it may be easy to ignore or discard many ideas of young people in your company, but if you listen carefully, you may just find new secrets to success. Especially if your business is faltering in any way, don't fall back on the tried and true. Listen to some of the younger generation's new ideas. Don't be too proud to consider their suggestions. They may be able to make what you are doing immeasurably better. Oh, sure, some youthful ideas may be too naïve or idealistic, but occasionally you will find a nugget that might just lead you to the mother lode. I know it happened for me!

Most people realize that change is inevitable, but instead of complaining about it or reminiscing about "the good old days," a Knockout Entrepreneur looks for ways to make change work for him, rather than against him. Change may jolt you out of your comfort zone, but as you embrace new and better ways to do what you do, your business or career will flourish.

KNOCKOUT IDEAS
TO STIMULATE YOUR SUCCESS

1. Are you mentally ready for change? Do you really want a better situation than the one you are currently experiencing?

2. Have your basic skills become dull or outdated? How might a refresher course help jump-start you on the road to success?

3. Is there any logical reason why your dreams cannot come true, why you cannot achieve your goal? If not, then decide today to renew your commitment to get the job done.

4. Honestly acknowledge that it may take months, possibly years of hard work and sacrifice, to allow your counterintuitive moves to bear fruit. But keep in mind that from this point on, you will be doing what you want to do in the way that is uniquely your own. The energy you will bring to the work you enjoy almost guarantees your success.

CHAPTER ELEVEN

SUCCESS COMES IN *CANS*

've seen so many people fail in business (and in life!) because of fear. Some people are afraid to go into business because they are afraid to take a risk, but even sadder to me, many entrepreneurs who have taken that first plunge often back away from their dreams because of an initial lack of success.

When I first began boxing, I didn't have a clue. I was a street fighter, a thug; I didn't have the foggiest idea about how to fight with finesse, how to pace myself, how to work with my strengths and overcome my weaknesses, or how to look for open shots in my opponents. I grew up in the Fifth Ward of Houston—we used to call it the Bloody Fifth because almost every weekend someone got shot, knifed, or killed. I never finished high school; come to think of it, I never finished junior high school. Instead, I dropped out of school and after hanging around the streets of Houston and getting in trouble, my mother and I finally agreed that I should join a new program the government had started called the Job Corps. In the Job Corps I learned a skill, but I also learned to box. At first I wasn't good at it, but I was a quick study.

With only eighteen amateur bouts under my belt, fighting in various cities around the United States, I entered the 1968 Olympic Games in Mexico City and won a gold medal. Back home in Houston, I wore that gold medal everywhere. Those were the days of Nehru jackets and big medallions, so I made my medal fit in with whatever I was wearing. I wore it so much that some of the gold began to rub off. Later a jeweler helped restore that medal for me, and I put it in a historical society in Texas so kids could see it and be inspired. The message I wanted them to get was that I came out of the Fifth Ward to do big things—you can too! I wanted all children and aspiring athletes to look at that medal as belonging to them as much as it does to my children. The first step toward being a success at anything is that you have to believe you can do it!

When Thomas Edison was working on the incandescent lightbulb, he failed time and time again. Some estimates say he tried more than two thousand times to make that light work. But rather than get discouraged and give up, he had the attitude: "I now know two thousand ways how *not* to make a lightbulb." And of course, you know the end of the story. Thomas Edison not only invented an incandescent lightbulb, but he also created ways that his invention could be used in homes and buildings.

To be successful in life, you must get in the habit of turning negatives into positives. Everybody loses at something sometime, but if you are afraid to take a risk, you'll never accomplish much. You can't always play safe or conservatively; sometimes you have to step out in faith. You have to put in extra effort if you hope to get something good out.

DEAL WITH REJECTION

I learned a great deal about stepping out in faith and dealing with rejection during my stint as a judge on the second season of the ABC television show *American Inventor*, one of *American Idol* producer Simon Cowell's spin-off shows. I joined the show's acerbic British judge, Peter Jones, along with Pat Croce, a retired NBA executive formerly with the Philadelphia 76ers, and Sara Blakely, an "undergarments entrepreneur," as she described herself. Sara is the creator of the Spanx line of products, worn under women's clothes to "hide and sleek," as she put it.

Similar to Cowell's highly successful program, the idea of *Inventor* was to conduct searches in a cross section of major American cities, including Los Angeles, New York, Houston, Chicago, San Francisco, and Tampa, giving inventors a chance to display their creations. Then we whittled down the contestants to six finalists, who were awarded $50,000 and one month to develop their products before the producers and judges narrowed the number of contestants to three for the grand finale.

It was a grueling schedule for all of us. We saw dozens of inventors display their wares in every city. We put in long days in the television studio and taped at least two shows each day. The trick, of course, was to be enthusiastic for both shows, no matter how long it took to get them done. It was tough to stay objective after a while, but I kept reminding myself that these people had poured their lives into their inventions, and some of them had truly stepped out in faith to get their product in the door. I knew rejection was going to be hard on all of them, but the attempt at success was worth a shot.

We saw all sorts of creative inventions during our tapings, such as Doggy Air Conditioners, Bullet Ball, and a Bladder Buddy. Some inventions were incredibly creative, some were just plain wacky, and some were a little of both.

The funniest invention was the one I called the Panther, although I guess the real name was the Black Cougar, a Batman-like superhero character created by a forty-nine-year-old filmmaker, Silvio DiSalvatore. Silvio had all four judges sitting on our chairs in awe, scratching our chins as he went through his energetic and slightly eccentric presentation telling us the Black Cougar could be used to protect kids. "A new superhero for a new generation of kids," Silvio declared. In his part New York Bronx, part Italian-sounding (I think) accent, Silvio told us that the Black Cougar was the greatest thing since Batman. He told how he had created a children's movie about a superhero—the Black Cougar—who saved a child from a kidnapping ring.

Silvio envisioned dolls, cartoons, action figures, and other products to go with the Black Cougar. "This is the one superhero whose only goal is to protect children," he kept repeating. He never quite explained how the Black Cougar was going to do that, but he was certainly passionate about his product. Meanwhile, the Black Cougar just stood in his costume, towering over the frenetic DiSalvatore. Everybody else on the judges' panel said he was a fool. I told him, "You're a star."

I had a hard time saying no to any of the contestants, even to the Panther, so I voted yes. Sara did too, but Pat and Peter voted thumbs down on the Black Cougar. Before he left the stage, I raised my fist and gave it a pump. "Go, Cougar," I called after him. Croce looked over at Sara and me and said, "You just said yes to a cat." But the audience loved DiSalvatore's zaniness, so the producers brought him back for a special appearance on our finale, even though he wasn't one of the finalists.

I wanted DiSalvatore and others to know: "You didn't fail; you didn't waste your time. You got it here. You demonstrated your product on national television. You never know who might see it and want that product. Just because you didn't win the contest doesn't mean that you didn't win."

During the last show, there were six finalists and three had to be eliminated. We finally got down to three contestants and someone asked me, "What do you think, George?"

"I'm not telling anyone no!"

Pat Croce piped up and said, "I'll do it!"

I looked back at him and said, "I'm so glad you are here."

The winner of the 2007 season finale was Greg Chavez, a fireman who invented a Guardian Angel sprinkler to put out a fire on a Christmas tree. It was just an idea! But he believed in it, and Greg gave a strong, moving presentation about how many fires began by faulty electrical wiring on Christmas tree decorations. He said the idea first occurred to him fifteen years earlier after seeing the news that a Christmas tree fire had claimed the life of a child. Fireman Chavez said he could never get over the image of that father carrying his child out of the burning home, and he said he vowed to do all that he could to make sure it never happened again.

Chavez described the sprinkler as a small, pressurized tank of water that looked like a Christmas gift placed under the tree and was attached to a small hose leading to the top of the Christmas tree. There a fusible link was disguised as an angel tree topper. An alarm was also placed on the tree to alert families in case of fire. First Alert bought the invention, and Chavez was awarded one million dollars in prize money. Ironically, Chavez's invention was just an idea; I never actually saw the thing work. But it was a great idea and the audience and the First Alert executives felt strongly that it had potential.

The runner-up prize went to Elaine Cato, a Realtor from Tennessee who invented a new type of bra, the Six-in-One Convertible Brassiere, that could be altered easily to be worn with various types of clothing, especially backless dresses. The well-known undergarment manufacturer Maidenform bought the product.

A schoolteacher from Oklahoma also had a great idea. Ricky DeRennaux entered HT Racers, his "custom build racers invention," as he described it.

Intended for kids nine years of age and up, it was a kit and a computer program that allowed kids to design and build their own remote-controlled vehicles. It looked like fun to me! Ricky didn't win the big money, but he did catch the attention of Spin Master, a company that offered to sponsor his product.

There was also a Wrap Away cabinet, a contraption that could be put in a drawer that allowed the dispensing of paper towels, gift wrap, or other products, and I thought the EZT4U, a basket for brewing tea in a standard electric quick-drip coffeemaker, was a good idea too. I had a hard time saying no to any of the inventors because I was so proud of them for taking their products as far as they had. But that is the nature of the show; it is a contest, and similar to a boxing match, somebody has to win and somebody has to lose.

Some products I really liked, but others I didn't care for as much. Some were just hard to believe. One of the saddest products I saw was a rather odd effort called the Squirrel Circus. A genial-looking fellow came on stage in Houston around eleven o'clock at night. It was the end of a very long day of auditions, and all the judges, including me, were extremely tired after viewing hours of inventions ranging from moderately strange to downright weird. It had been that kind of day.

To the man's left stood his invention, an odd assortment of sticks, rope, something that looked like a bird feeder, and some plastic tubing, all in various crossbar shapes connected to each other.

"Hi, my name is Jeff Miller, and this is the Squirrel Circus." He pointed to the contraption as though it was one of the Seven Wonders of the World. Jeff then explained that one day he was looking out the kitchen window of his home in Cutchogue, New York, when he saw a squirrel trying to get into the family's backyard bird feeder. The squirrel was doing leaps and flips and finally made it.

"And that's when I had the idea that is changing the course of the war between humans and squirrels!" Jeff proclaimed. I knew I was tired, but to tell the truth, I hadn't known there was such a war going on. Then I recalled what a problem it was sometimes keeping squirrels out of the animals' food, and I smiled in understanding. That was probably a mistake because my response seemed to energize Jeff even more.

"I realized our yard was full of acrobats!" Jeff gushed. "All they needed was a place to perform. They needed a Squirrel Circus!" Jeff gestured again in the direction of the five-foot-tall, four-foot-wide odd assortment of sticks and tubes on the stage. "It's a jungle gym for squirrels," Jeff said, "including a trapeze and a springboard, on which squirrels perform to get food. It actually works." Jeff looked at us as though we should have been in awe by then. I was just tired and I could tell that Croce and Jones were getting surly. Sara was nodding, but I couldn't tell if it was from interest or lack of sleep.

"The squirrels came and did their amazing stunts on the Squirrel Circus, and left our bird feeder alone," Jeff said triumphantly. "There!"

Sara was nodding again, so Jeff riveted her attention with his final statement. "The Squirrel Circus really does what our slogan says: It Turns Pests into Performers!"

In his typical British flare, Peter Jones shifted in his seat and then said bluntly, "But it's just a bunch of sticks!"

I really felt badly for Jeff Miller and his Squirrel Circus, not simply because he was rejected from the contest, but because everyone made such fun of him, and I could see the hurt in his face. He obviously believed in the potential of his invention, and apparently his family had enjoyed watching the squirrels play on the . . . ah . . . bunch of sticks, so I hated to see him disappointed. But he didn't stand a chance, especially at that hour of night. I hope that Jeff and his family members are still enjoying his Squirrel Circus in their backyard. I respect him for following his dream.

When you are a Knockout Entrepreneur, win or lose, you have to pick up and go on. If somebody rejects your product or service, don't take it personally.

It is not a rejection of *you* necessarily. You are not a reject; rejection happens. Failure is part of the success process. Losing often leads to winning. Sometimes you can throw your best punch and miss. When I first started boxing, sometimes I would swing so hard that I'd spin around, miss my opponent, and nearly fall out of the ring. Sure, I felt silly, but I just regained my footing and kept right on swinging.

No matter how many times you experience rejection, a Knockout Entrepreneur knows that acceptance is right around the corner. If one idea doesn't work, something else will. Knockout Entrepreneurs understand that "success comes in *cans*"; we focus on what we *can* do rather than what we cannot. We choose to look at what we have left, rather than what we have lost. A Knockout Entrepreneur understands that isolated instances of defeat or failure are only stepping-stones to long-term success.

KNOCKOUT IDEAS
TO STIMULATE YOUR SUCCESS

1. People who are highly successful refuse to play it safe. Often they go out on a limb and take a chance of embarrassing themselves. What idea for a new product or service or business has been percolating in your mind for some time? What is keeping you from daring to do something unorthodox?

2. Truly successful people rarely achieve their goals by luck. They advance by thinking through their options, weighing each one, making a decision or a commitment, and then stepping into the future with confidence. Begin today to make thoughtful, careful, incremental steps in the direction of your goals. End the debate within yourself

and *do* something that will take you closer to seeing your dream fulfilled.

3. What are some factors that might cause you to be overly cautious? Of what are you afraid regarding the next step toward success? Recognize that every great success story has a background of rejection. Yours will too, but you must accept that. Overcome your reticence to step out in faith; do what you believe you were born to do.

CHAPTER TWELVE

MAKE THE MOST OF WHAT YOU HAVE

n 1983, I used what remained of my life savings to open a gym, the George Foreman Youth and Community Center, in the inner-city of Houston, where kids could come to play, work out, and train to become boxers. When I ran out of money at the youth center, I didn't want to beg for operating funds, so I went back to boxing to earn enough money to keep the doors open. At first nobody cared. I was just another former champion trying to make a comeback. I didn't have enough money to advertise, and reporters didn't want to interview me. But every once in a while, a sportscaster on a television station would give me about ten seconds. I made sure that I took advantage of every opportunity to promote my fights. *Ten seconds? Okay, I'm going to fill every second with something good!* I thought. The interviewer would ask a simple question like,

"George, do you really think you can regain your title now that you are in your forties?"

That was all the opening I needed. "Yes, sir," I crowed with a big smile on my face. "Yes, I'm forty," I yelled. "I'm George Foreman. I used to be heavyweight champion of the world, and I can do it again. If I miss you with my left, if I miss you with my right, I'll belly bump you. Boom!" I said, grabbing my waist and thrusting it forward. Always with a smile. Ten seconds. And the audiences loved it. People began calling their local stations and even their networks, asking to see more of me.

Before long, Madison Avenue was calling on me to do television commercials. I hesitated at first, but I finally decided I could do the commercials without compromising my integrity if I did ads only for products in which I truly believed. I've been pitching products ever since.

Salton, the company that makes the George Foreman grill, was a little-known home appliance manufacturer before we put together our deal for the George Foreman Lean, Mean, Fat-Reducing Grilling Machine. The company's claim to fame prior to that had been an espresso and coffee maker, and two waterproof radios—one for the shower and one for the pool. But they had created a new type of slanted electric grill, and we struck a deal. They were great folks, but they didn't have a lot of money to advertise. Again, we took advantage of every opportunity to promote the grill.

Initially our sales for the grill were sluggish at best. In 1996, we sold about two hundred thousand units—not bad, but not good either. Some stores hinted that they might quit carrying it because it wasn't selling. But when people actually bought the grill, they loved it. People ran up to me in airports and called out my name. I thought, *They must have seen my last fight five months ago.* I'd never had so many people smiling at me. But that wasn't the case. They said, "George, we love your grill."

I thought that was rather interesting. When I had done KFC commercials, occasionally people would say, "Boy, George, I loved that commercial. That was really funny." But nobody ever came up to me and said, "Boy, George, I just love that chicken you advertise." Nor had they said much about the McDonald's burger, or the Meineke mufflers, or any other product I endorsed. But everywhere I went, people couldn't wait to tell me about how much they loved the grill.

In the mid-1990s, when the George Foreman grill was first starting to take off in popularity, I appeared on the QVC network. I bantered back and forth with the QVC hosts, and we talked about the grill and how it worked. We showed how sleek it was and how easy it was to clean, and even demon-strated how to cook on the grill. Suddenly, the phones lit up. So many people were calling that the QVC phone banks were jammed and callers couldn't order fast enough. Every available QVC employee grabbed a phone and started taking orders.

Leon Dreimann, Salton's CEO, studied the videotape to see what magic words somebody had said that had caused the sudden avalanche of sales. As he reviewed the tape, Leon started laughing at what he saw. While the QVC hosts were busy talking about the George Foreman grill and plugging the product, I had spotted some fresh burgers they had just finished cooking. Without really thinking much about it, I had grabbed a hamburger bun, placed a still sizzling, juicy burger on it, and started munching. When the camera panned in my direction, I just raised my eyebrows as if to say, "It's good!" And I launched into my own version of the Mr. Ice Cream Show. "I got this grill! I got hamburgers!" I wanted the audience to know that I didn't just sell the product; I used it. That might have been the best burger I ever ate because sales of the George Foreman grill skyrocketed as a result of that visit to QVC.

For the next three to four years, Salton couldn't make George Foreman grills fast enough. QVC alone sold more than 1.5 million units. Suddenly, Salton was on *Fortune*'s annual list of 100 Fastest-Growing Companies, with

173

sales increasing every year—$183 million in 1997, $506 million in 1999, $792 million in 2001, $922 million in 2002, and the sales keep going. We didn't have a lot of money to advertise when we first started, but we used what we had—our time and our talent.

You may not have a lot of money to advertise your business or services, but if you will use what you do have—your time, talent, perseverance, or willingness to work—and promote what you are doing with enthusiasm and confidence, you will attract attention.

IF YOU DON'T HAVE A LASER, USE A SHOTGUN

I like the shotgun theory when it comes to being a Knockout Entrepreneur. Rather than put all my hopes and dreams on one shot, I prefer to scatter a lot of shots out there. It takes only one to bring down the prize.

When I was just a little boy, my uncle went hunting not for sport but as a way to help feed his family. Some hunters preferred to buy expensive bullets; they were the sharpshooters. But my uncle always bought a bunch of cheap buckshot. Anytime he pulled that trigger, he knew that he had a family back home depending on him to hit a target. He couldn't afford to wait for the perfect opportunity. He had hungry mouths to feed. So he sprayed that buckshot out there, and he usually brought something home for his family's dinner table (although they did have to pick buckshot out of the meat occasionally).

In business, that shotgun approach means that I'm going to have deals going all the time. I go after everything, spraying "shots" in every direction. I don't wait for a single perfect opportunity. I don't hone in with laserlike intensity on any one idea until I'm ready to pour myself into it. I'm constantly working on new ideas, looking at new inventions, new business opportunities created by other people who want me to become involved in their success. I throw a lot of buckshot out there. Maybe only one will hit the target, or maybe I'll hit several targets. Some of them will be great and yield a tremendous return. Others may fall through, and I'll have wasted a shot or two. But in my view, you have to spend some money to make some money. You have to invest some time and effort if you hope to receive a good return. Some people say, "My ship just hasn't come in yet," but the truth is, they've never sent a ship *out*!

GIVE A LITTLE—GAIN A LOT

Sometimes you have to give up a little to gain a lot. This takes humility, and it also requires you to trust the person with whom you are working. A young man came to me with a new exercise glove that looked similar to a boxing glove. The young fellow showed me all the features of the glove and then asked me to endorse it and allow my name to be on it. I examined the glove and I thought that it had potential, so I introduced the young man to the people who handle my product development and they offered him a 5 percent share of the profits off the market price.

"Five percent!" the young man protested. "It's my idea. It's my glove. I just want George to put his name on it. I should be offering you 5 percent."

"Okay, fine," my product development man told him. "Keep your glove and you can design, manufacture, advertise, and market it yourself. And you can keep 100 percent of the profits."

That's what the young man did. But the young man failed to understand the potential of the George Foreman Exercise Glove and how it could be marketed all over the world with my name on it. With his name on it, the chances of a major manufacturer picking up the product were substantially less. Yes, he could keep 100 percent of his profits, but 100 percent of nothing is still nothing. He'd have been much better off to receive 5 percent of a potentially large amount of profits. But to do that, he would have had to humble himself, and his unwillingness to do so probably cost him a fortune.

Everyone wants to say, "*I* did this! *I* created that. This is *my* product. *I* designed that."

I learned a long time ago that to be successful, I had to keep my *I* out of the way. Leave the *I* alone because the big *I* will lead to the poor house. Somebody said, "In the middle of every sin is a big *I*." That's probably true; most sin happens because somebody says, "I want what I want and I want it my way and I want it now." Focusing on *I . . . I . . . I . . .* will get you in trouble every time.

You can design, develop, and market a new idea for a product, but it will be much easier if you can find a George Foreman, a Chuck Norris, a company like Nike, or someone who can get your product in front of a larger audience. Yes, that may take some humility on your part, but it will pay huge dividends in the future.

I experienced this when we took the George Foreman grill to Asia. We had already sold more than one hundred million George Foreman grills, but the company decided to spend a lot of money to market the grill in China. The CEO said, "Okay, George, we're going to make an infomercial featuring Jackie Chan and you. So we're going to say it is the Jackie Chan / George Foreman Grill."

My natural reaction was, *Jackie Chan? I know Jackie is a successful martial artist with his style of kung fu, he's been in a slew of movies, and he's a real nice fellow, but I don't need Jackie to sell a grill!*

But wait a minute. Jackie Chan is a living icon, known to millions and millions of people in Asia. He's a singer and an actor, and he has all sorts of video games built on his characters. He has funded numerous schools around the world, including schools in China, for poor children. He is a positive role model in many ways. In 2006, he pledged up to half his assets to charity work upon his death. Why shouldn't I work with Jackie Chan? Who cares whose name is on the grill? By working together we can reach more than a billion new potential customers!

On a promotional tour, I noticed that Jackie was loved all over Asia. He speaks several Asian languages. The promoters showed us the billboards featuring "Jackie Chan and George Foreman" that were planned for East Asia. Why do I need Jackie Chan? Because he is successful and he can help make our product even more successful.

Pride often gets in the way. *Why do I need that person? What's wrong with me? This is my product.* That voice of pride can rob you of a great opportunity if you are not careful.

Now when I go to China or another Asian country, people will know me. They may say, "Oh, I have that Jackie Chan / George Foreman grill," but that's okay with me. We're doing something similar with the grill in Mexico and in South America, working out deals and partnerships in which I may not own 100 percent, but the numbers of pieces of product will increase exponentially. Being flexible and keeping my ego in check will lead to increased profitability for me and far greater distribution of our products worldwide.

TIME IS MONEY

Many inventors and entrepreneurs spend a lot of their own money trying to create a great product; or once they have perfected it, they spend their life savings trying to get their product to market. No question about it, research and development, advertising, and marketing take major cash pools nowadays. Financial grants are available for certain products. Perhaps your product would interest the government or a particular industry having to do with national security, medicine, scientific research, or other public benefit. You may be able to get a research and development grant while you work on the project.

But for most products or services, you will have to come up with the financing on your own or find someone else who believes in your product and sees it as a worthwhile investment. Beware of rip-offs, though, books and audio–video series touting the fact that if you will just follow their formulas, you too can have an overflowing pot full of free money. Usually the only people who get rich on those deals are the people selling the books or audio–video series. There are helpful, reliable resources available to entrepreneurs, but unfortunately, there are more than a few shysters, preying on your dreams, knowing that you would do almost anything to see your idea take root and grow. In most cases you will probably have to spend your own money to attend a seminar where other successful entrepreneurs can share their tried and tested ideas with you, as well as their more speculative ventures. Buy quality business books written by successful entrepreneurs, and read them! They won't help you a bit just sitting on your bookshelf or coffee table. You must get the information inside your head and heart if you expect it to reap any dividends in your bank account.

But wait a minute. Frequently, you won't have to spend nearly as much of your money if you are willing to spend your time and effort. Good old-fashioned elbow grease can sometimes get your product out to the public.

There's an old saying "time is money," and that is true in many ways. Time is the one commodity that will always be in limited supply, so choose wisely how you spend it, and make the most of it. Most successful entrepreneurs put in ten to twelve hours per day at their work, but not all make good use of those hours. Many entrepreneurs waste enormous amounts of time responding to random or unplanned phone calls, reading the newspaper, answering e-mails, checking the mail, or paying bills. All of these things may *seem* urgent, but do they really enhance your productivity? Are they part of your plan to sell something today? Could they be done during a less "prime" time? Too often, entrepreneurs are trapped by the tyranny of the urgent, doing things that seem important at the moment, but don't really advance their business.

Instead spend the majority of your working hours doing something that moves your business ahead. Ask yourself honestly, as a boss would an employee, *Are you giving your business a full day's worth of productive work?* As you examine your work routine and discover that you are doing things that don't really contribute a great deal to your future success and wealth, you must make the appropriate adjustments in your schedule. For instance, I heard about one man who answers e-mails only early in the morning or late at night, but not during business hours. Maybe keeping up with the local news is an important aspect of your business, but you could read the paper each evening after dinner rather than early in your business day. You might be amazed at how much more successful you become by making a few minor adjustments in your schedule.

Following are a few more miscellaneous secrets to help you along the way to becoming a Knockout Entrepreneur.

DRESS FOR SUCCESS

Look successful, even if you aren't—yet. Always dress slightly better than the occasion demands. You don't need to overdo it, but whether we like to admit it or not, there is still a business "uniform" that is accepted in places where money talks. Discover what that uniform is in your line of work and invest in it. If you're not sure what the norm is for a particular business with whom you want to work, visit that business's Web site; if it has a corporate magazine, scan through the pages and observe the images presented; or if possible, stop by the business location as people are entering or exiting the workplace and notice how the people are dressed. If in your clothing style you stray too far from what you see, you will make a statement, but it may not be a positive reflection on you.

DON'T OBSESS

Have a life outside of work; don't sacrifice your family or friends on the altar of success. We say that so often that it almost seems trite. No business or career is worth losing your loved ones as a result of your success.

Get away from the business every so often. Have a hobby or participate in a community activity with your church or the local Little League program or something that gives you an outlet away from work. I love cars. I have a couple dozen of them, and each one is special to me. I love animals too, and I enjoy watching them, playing with them, learning from them. Your hobby doesn't have to be expensive or time consuming, but it helps to keep you sane and honest by getting you away from work for a while. Go out for a cup of coffee for no reason. Take off one day out of seven as a Sabbath; you'll work better and more effectively the other six days of the week.

READ FOR SUCCESS

It is not a coincidence that nearly all the highly successful people I know or know about are readers. Most of them are avid readers. When someone tells me, "Oh, George, I'm really not much of a reader," that statement tells me quite a bit about that person. As a young man, I developed a taste for reading and I still find rich nuggets of truth in books. In fact, when I left boxing and became a preacher, I took all the televisions out of our home. I wanted to make a clean break with my past and create a new environment. For ten years we did not watch television in the Foreman home, and to tell you the truth, I didn't miss it.

I never stopped reading, though. In the past I mostly read magazines, but now I read more books. Even when Joan and I didn't have much money, I'd buy books at used bookstores. First one book, then another; soon I was reading several books a month, then several books each week. Since we no longer had a television, often at night I'd read a book aloud to Joan. She enjoyed my reading to her, I learned so much, and my horizons expanded immensely.

When I went back into boxing, I wanted to study the tapes of potential opponents so I rented a television and videotape player. Joan came in one day and said, "George Foreman, you're watching television."

"No, no, no, Joan," I said sheepishly. "I'm studying boxing videos."

"That makes no difference to me. You're watching television!"

Within a few days, we not only had a new television in our home, but it was a large-screen TV, complete with cable. Needless to say, our reading time has been greatly reduced. But I still take time to read, and I encourage my family members to read.

To this day I'm always buying books for my sons and daughters or suggesting books they can read. I recommend stories of great businessmen and businesswomen for my kids. I want them to see how other people have used their gifts and talents to make a way in this world. I'm glad my children are readers. They enjoy my stories, and I am usually quick to pass them on, but sometimes a book can inspire them in ways that I cannot. Nobody can take away the education you receive by reading great books.

If I could give you one piece of advice that would make you more successful, I'd say *read*. Reading does for your mind what physical exercise does for your body. If a regimen of physical self-improvement is important to your success, how much more so is a regimen of self-improvement for your brain. Neglect a good mental diet and your mental sharpness atrophies; challenge it, exercise it, and it will develop strength. Cut down on your consumption of mental junk food, information you can't use to improve your life, and read books, magazines, newsletters, trade publications, and anything that pertains to the business you hope to do. Read widely and always ask yourself, *Do these publications provide me with the information I need to accomplish my goals?* If not, then you may need to adjust your list.

Walking into a bookstore or a library can be a bit overwhelming if you don't know what you are looking for. So how do you know where to start and what to read? I like to ask successful people what they are reading. Rarely does a person who is thriving in his or her career and personal life respond, "George, I'm not reading anything right now." Usually, it is just the opposite. Successful people are almost always reading something to expand their horizons. If you don't know where to start, ask someone whose life and career you admire for some suggestions.

I like to read books about people who have accomplished great things, especially things I hope to do. When I was thinking about coming back as a boxer, I read Archie Moore's book *Any Boy Can*, and it inspired me in my midforties to work toward winning the world heavyweight boxing championship for the second time. Archie had been in my corner when I beat Joe Frazier to become the heavyweight champion of the world in 1973. He had been the recipient of all sorts of "over the hill" jokes as a boxer; he fought his last fight as a pro in 1965 at age fifty-two. When I read Archie's book, I thought, *If Archie can fight at fifty-two, I'm not too old in my forties.* Reading that book made a profound impression on my life.

Today many people tend to read less; they think they can get the information they need more quickly on the Internet or from cable television services.

New technologies will continue to open new horizons in the information world, but nothing will stimulate your business ideas like reading. Besides that, reading will give you a leg up on your competition, since most of your competitors don't read as much as they should. Others read only to escape reality or to catch up on the latest scandal or the most recent Hollywood celebrity meltdown. In most cases that sort of reading will not help your business and will, in fact, be a detriment to you since it is keeping you from expanding your horizons by reading quality materials.

Think about it: if you spent the next six months reading everything you could find about your business, career, or family goals, wouldn't your confidence level rise, your knowledge and abilities increase, and your performance improve? Maybe by reading about your chosen field, you will discover new techniques or greater opportunities that depend not on learning new skills but on doing better what you already do.

Steve, a successful cinematographer, buys books and magazines almost every time he travels through an airport. "I like to scan the magazines to see what is new, what new trends are coming," he said. "I read books for inspiration, but I also read books for innovation. Sometimes I find just the right idea I was looking for as I am reading about somebody else's techniques."

As the great motivational speaker Charlie "Tremendous" Jones (he always responded, "Tremendous!" when people asked him how he was doing) used to say, "You are the same today as you'll be in five years except for two things: the people you meet and the books you read."[1] Keep expanding your horizons and you will be amazed at how new ideas or new opportunities keep coming your direction.

Knockout Entrepreneurs don't sit around whining about what they don't have or can't do. They are constantly on the lookout for new ways to make the most of what they do have. An amazing phenomenon often occurs. As you use what you have, you seem to attract more. Make the most of what you have by using your talents, dressing as the successful person you want to become, and constantly expanding your mind through insights you have gained by reading great books. Before long, people will be looking to you for advice on how to become a Knockout Entrepreneur!

KNOCKOUT IDEAS
TO STIMULATE YOUR SUCCESS

1. What resources do you have at your disposal right now that you are not putting to full use? Think in terms of the special abilities and skills that you have; consider how you are using your spare time. How can you better use your time and talents in ways that will move you forward on your journey to success?

2. A limited vocabulary will limit your success. On the other hand, one of the easiest ways to improve your vocabulary and communication skills is to read good books. In the past six months, what books have you read? How have those books helped or hindered your quest for success?

3. It is often said that words are powerful. During the next week, attempt to learn one new word each day. You can open the dictionary and choose a word that you don't know, or you can go to several free word services available online. Take advantage of these resources, and you will be amazed how doors open more quickly in your journey toward success, happiness, and significance.

CHAPTER THIRTEEN

KEEP ANSWERING THE BELL

I n boxing matches, you are often tired, thirsty, and hurting. You don't think you can stand up and take one more blow, but you keep answering the bell. When the bell sounds indicating the next round, you get back into the ring; you keep going. Sometimes your head is hurting and your vision is blurred, and occasionally, you even get knocked down. But the key to success in boxing—or in any area of life—is to keep getting back up. It is no shame to take a blow, lose your balance or perspective, and hit the floor. There is no dishonor in being knocked down. Dishonor comes only when you don't force yourself to get back up—especially when you *can* get back up, but you refuse to do it.

In 1974, I was boxing Muhammad Ali in Africa when I took a hard shot and was knocked to the floor. My manager, Dick Sadler, had always drilled into my mind, "If you ever get knocked down, don't try to get up too quickly. Look around the ring. Find me," he'd say. "And let me do the counting." Dick's reasoning was simple: sometimes when a boxer gets hit with such a powerful blow that it knocks him to the canvas, he attempts to get up too quickly, and he stumbles and falls over backward. Or if he doesn't allow enough time for the blow to pass, he gets up, and his opponent floors him again. So Dick and I always had a policy. If I got knocked down, I would stay put and look for Dick. He would do the counting, letting me know when it was time to get back up. Then I'd bound to my feet and the fight would continue. Of course, Dick never had to worry too much about using our plan because I didn't get knocked down very often. Usually I was the guy doing the knocking down!

But in Africa in 1974, Ali caught me with a powerful, solid blow, and I hit the floor. Rather than bounce back to my feet, I did just as we had always planned. I stayed on the mat for a few seconds, allowing my head to clear as I looked for Dick. I caught his eye and watched for his signal that it was time to get up. But something went horribly wrong. I was on the floor, but I was not listening to the count. I was watching Dick. By the time Dick signaled me to get up, the ref had rattled off a quick, "Eight, nine, ten!" The fight was over, and I had lost! I had been technically knocked out, even though I had the strength, the ability, and the will to get back up.

I was embarrassed and angry: angry at Dick for not getting me up in time, and most of all, angry at myself for not listening to the count. I hurt inside, not from physical pain, but from the embarrassment and revulsion I felt at losing that way. I was lower than low. The knowledge that I had not been beaten—but that I had actually beaten myself by not getting up in time— lurked constantly in the back of my mind. I said, "I will never allow that to happen to me again."

Less than two years later, I was fighting Ron Lyle in Las Vegas. I had not fought since losing to Muhammad Ali in the famous Rumble in the Jungle on October 29, 1974, in Kinshasa, Zaire. Well, that's not quite accurate; there was that one day in Toronto the previous April when I took on five opponents in one evening in exhibition fights. After losing to Ali, I was mad enough to take on the world—and I tried to do just that! But Ron Lyle was my first official bout after fighting Ali, and I was primed and ready.

Lyle, ranked number five at the time, had twenty-nine victories under his belt, twenty of which were knockouts. A former gang member, Lyle was an intimidating, almost sinister-looking fighter, having spent seven and a half years in prison where he had once been declared clinically dead after a prison brawl. He was a vicious boxer whom Muhammad Ali had barely beaten in the eleventh round.

Our bout in Vegas started a little slow, with both of us sizing each other up. Then suddenly near the end of the first round, Lyle caught me with a hard right that nearly knocked my trunks off! I mean that man could punch! After that we went after each other like two bull moose locked in battle. It was about the closest thing to a street fight that I had been in since I had begun boxing professionally.

I came back strong in rounds two and three, and by the end of the third, Lyle's eye was beginning to puff. But that didn't bother him a bit. It just made him madder. He came after me hard in the fourth, and when he stunned me with a strong right-hand punch early in the round, followed by a series of uppercuts and hooks, I hit the floor, facedown, landing on my head as though I were trying out a new yoga position. Man, that Lyle could hit.

Weak and embarrassed, I could hear the crowd cheering, but whether they were hoping I'd get back up or stay down, I didn't know. I looked around for Dick Sadler to see what he was doing. Most of all, I couldn't believe that it had happened again. Here I was down on the canvas again. Worse yet, I knew that Lyle would be salivating now; he could taste victory as he looked at me on the mat. I knew that getting up meant that I was going

187

to get clobbered again; I knew I couldn't stop him from coming at me, and this man's punches packed some wallop!

Then I remembered how I felt that night in Africa when I should have gotten up, could have gotten up, but didn't. I said to myself, *Today, I may die, but I must get up*. I couldn't see very well, and I knew that Lyle would come at me with full force again, but I said to myself in those moments on the floor, *I never again want to live with the knowledge that I could have gotten up and didn't. I don't want to look myself in the mirror and hear me saying, "You didn't get back up."*

So I slowly mustered my strength and staggered to my feet. I was hurting, but I said, *If I am up, I might as well keep fighting*. I was also mad. I didn't dare let Lyle get away with that, so I went after him and connected with a powerful right that Lyle must have thought was a lightning bolt; I hit him so hard that the blow dislodged his mouthpiece. I quickly followed up with a left hook that knocked Lyle all the way under the lowest rope. Most guys that I hit that hard never bothered to get back up. Except for Ron Lyle.

Not only did he get up, but he came back at me with a look in his eye that said, "All right, George. It's my turn."

And it was! I mean he decked me with a tremendous left-right combination that knocked me off balance, and I keeled over onto my shoulder, then onto my face. I was down for the second time in the same fight! Fortunately I was saved by the bell ending the round.

I made my way over to my corner and sat down on my stool to rest a minute. Later in my comeback years, in my quest for a second world heavyweight title, I never sat down between rounds. I'd stand up all through the break, and my standing while my opponent was sitting on his stool made a statement to my opponent: "Oh my, that George Foreman must not even be tired. Look at him standing over there, and I can barely sit up on my stool."

But in 1976, although I was in much better shape, I still sat down on the corner stool for a rest between rounds. Gil Clancy, my cornerman, splashed water on my face as he read me the riot act. "Lyle is hurt," Gil told me. "And you're hurt."

I knew that much. He didn't have to tell me that! I looked back at Gil blankly without saying a word.

Then Gil said something really significant: "George, the one that's gonna win is the one who wants it most." Gil stuck his forefinger on my chest. "Do you want it most?"

"Sure I do, Gil," I mumbled.

I stood up and went out for the fifth round, meeting Lyle head-on in the middle of the ring. We exchanged a series of hard blows and then I caught Lyle with a left hook, again knocking his mouthpiece completely out of his mouth. I kept after him, landing one hard punch after another until Lyle pitched forward and fell over on his face. I stepped back. I knew that when a man falls on his face, he rarely gets up. Lyle stayed on the canvas, and I was declared the winner.

That was one of the toughest boxing matches I'd ever fought, and I truly believe the turning point came when Lyle knocked me down and I forced myself to get back up. I won that fight by a knockout, not because I was so much better of a boxer than Ron Lyle, but because I kept getting back up. From then on I knew that if I could just make it to the next day, the next month, or the next year, I could make it, no matter what blows life threw at me.

I've applied that same principle in business. A number of my entrepreneurial business ventures have not proved nearly as successful as I had hoped. There have been plenty of times when I have attempted to achieve a goal, but failed, got knocked down, and had to struggle to get back up. Sure, the temptation is to say, "Oh, I think I'm just going to stay down for a while. At least while I'm down here on the canvas, nobody else is going to hit me." But you don't dare stay down. And the truth is, if you allow yourself to remain down for long, somebody might just come along and run over you! You better get up while you can!

A WILL TO WIN

Great fighters have a stubborn will to win that seems to carry them through obstacles or opposition that other people might legitimately regard as devastating setbacks. Champions constantly employ tactics designed to intimidate and impose their will on their opponents, whether it is showing a grim expression during the prefight face-off, standing up between rounds, looming over the opponent after knocking him down, taking hard hits and giving them right back without hesitation, refusing to step back despite the blows, or bouncing up and down on his toes during the break between the eleventh and twelfth rounds when his opponent is watching. All of these things are intended to do one thing—keep you alive!

In your career, as in boxing, you must maintain a never-give-up attitude. You may take some shots. You may get knocked down, but don't allow yourself to stay down. As long as you have a puff of air still left in you, get back up and give it another go. You just never know when that extra effort is going to bring you the victory you have been seeking.

The most important step is the one you decide to take to get back on your feet again. You can do it; don't let anyone tell you that you can't. I first became heavyweight champ of the world in 1973 as a young man; I was only twenty-four years of age. I won the heavyweight boxing championship again in November 1994 at the age of forty-five. If I could become the heavyweight champ of the world after being retired from the sport for ten years, you can do anything you want.

All you have to do is want it and work for it. Don't just talk about it; get up and do it. Don't listen to those who tell you it can't be done. If the world listened to those people, nothing would ever get done. Believe in God; believe in yourself. Believe that with His help, you can do anything you put your mind to doing. You have to be flexible; you can't be headstrong. But you can make it work. There is nothing wrong with being down, because you can only go up. But there is a lot wrong about being knocked down and staying down. And no matter what anybody tells you, it is never too late to start doing what you love, and it is never too late to start over again! Get up and do it!

Persistence is the name of the game for most of us who want to be successful. Ask people you know who are successful how they achieved their goals. You may be surprised to discover that it is rarely brilliant planning that brings success or significance. Neither does significance come as a result of having blind luck, winning the lottery (which I don't recommend that you play), or clever plotting. No, success usually comes to the persistent person.

Are you a fighter? Are you willing to endure pain or make sacrifices to see your dreams come true? If you are not, I hate to be the one to inform you of this, but you can be almost certain that your dreams will die before they are fulfilled. Victory and success usually come to the person who refuses to quit. More than any other single quality essential for success, persistence will be necessary for you to endure to the end. The character within you causes you to get back up after being knocked down ten times. That deep desire within gives you the extra oomph to keep going; it is the strength to persevere when you're not sure you can take another blow. It is the faith that will help you through the night in hopes that a better tomorrow will soon be here.

Too many people quit too soon, or more specifically, they quit just as soon as they can or when it seems completely reasonable in the eyes of other people. They are more concerned about what other people might think or say than they are about pursuing their dreams. But if you really want to be successful, commit in advance in your heart and mind and will that *I will not give up. I'm going to keep going until I win or God directs me to do otherwise.* That's a secret to success.

That sort of persistence is more important in determining your success or failure than any other single factor. It is more important than your ability, intelligence, skills, physical attractiveness, or anything else. You can lack almost all of the other so-called advantages in life and still be enormously successful if you have the determination never to give up. Many times your sheer persistence will compensate for what you lack in other areas of life.

AVOID TAKING A ROUND OFF

In boxing, a fight is twelve rounds; there are no ties and no overtimes. Every moment of every fight, you are on your way to either victory or defeat. Worse yet, you really don't know the score until the end of the boxing match. That's why, although a fighter may approach various rounds differently, every round is important. The third round is just as important as the eleventh round because the judges score each round individually. A smart boxer never takes a round off because in most cases, a round off—a round in which you may still be in the ring, but are not giving it your best shots—will be a lost round.

A great football player knows that he must play all four quarters of the game with the same intensity or risk losing. A tennis player knows she can't afford to relax or the match can turn around in a matter of seconds. Perhaps you've heard an athlete say, "We just have to give it everything we have. We can't afford to slough off."

In your career, your business, or any aspect of life, if you take a day off, you can be sure you are taking a loss. Certainly we need time for rest and recreation in our lives, and we all need a Sabbath—one day out of seven during which we do not work, but focus on our God and our family, a day to be refreshed and revitalized. Those opportunities need to be planned into our schedules.

Any other time, however, when you are supposed to be working, to the extent that you use that time for something else, you should recognize that you are falling behind. You are cheating yourself or somebody else. If you work in an office from 8:00 a.m. till 5:00 p.m., but you spend a half hour to an hour each day making personal phone calls, sending personal e-mails, or forwarding funny stories or jokes that have nothing to do with your business, you are taking a round off. You are also robbing your employer. If you are taking an extra fifteen minutes for lunch each day, you are taking a round off.

You can bet your bottom dollar that when you take that time off, somebody else is looking to take your spot. He may not do it all at once, in a knockout blow; but incrementally, as you slack off, someone else will be picking up ground, taking it one piece at a time, just as a boxer chips away at his opponent, racking up one point at a time. Opportunities are never really lost; *you* may have lost them, but someone else will come along to pick them up!

Can you take a round off and still win? Of course, but you must recognize that you have willfully given away points to the opposition, and now you must make up for lost time. Regaining the lead is not always as easy as it sounds, especially when you have fanned the flames of desire in your opponent by allowing an open shot or by providing an opportunity to make headway while you are cruising. When you take a round off, it is like waving a red flag in front of a bull. You are practically goading your competitors to stretch more for the lead.

If you have been coasting lately, wake up and notice what is happening. Inattention to details that really matter can cost you much more than you think. Don't wait another day; today is the time to get yourself back up to full steam ahead.

ACKNOWLEDGE WHEN YOU ARE WRONG

Sometimes the hardest words in the world to say are "I'm sorry, I was wrong. I made a mistake." But most Knockout Entrepreneurs—even highly successful ones—make their share of errors.

Have you ever flown in a private jet? Today many businesses rely on private aircraft to whisk their executives around the world at a moment's notice. But back in 1963, the private jet industry was just catching on, thanks to the tremendous efforts of one of the most prolific inventors in America, Bill Lear. Bill had been coming up with innovative ideas all of his life—he invented the first practical car radio, which he eventually sold to a company that came to be known as Motorola. He later invented eight-track tapes, a steam turbine to power cars and buses, and numerous other electronic gizmos. Bill's formal education was rather limited. He attended school only to the eighth grade, although he later took classes while in the navy, where he served as a radio operator. He did have an interesting sense of humor; he and his wife named one of their daughters Shanda—Shanda Lear, as in *chandelier*. (I wonder if people asked Bill about that name as often as they ask me about naming all my boys George.)

Quirky and at times hard to work with, Bill nonetheless could sure make an idea fly. At a time when most businessmen were traveling by commercial airliners and raving about how rapidly they could get from New York to Los Angeles aboard a DC-8, Bill Lear created an eight-seat private aircraft that would streak across the country at nearly six hundred miles per hour, flying at heights around forty thousand feet, and priced lower than his competitors. The Learjet soon became the most coveted sign of success among many corporate executives.

But one of the little-known stories about Bill's company is that even after it was flying high, it nearly flew apart. Bill and his wife, Moya, had put everything they had into getting that first Learjet off the ground in 1963. By 1966, they had sold fifty-five of the sleek new jets with orders for more than a dozen more.

Then tragedy struck. Within one month, two Learjets crashed and people lost their lives. Both crashes were odd in that they took place shortly after takeoff as the plane was rapidly ascending. This was especially troubling to Bill Lear, since one of his jet's exceptional characteristics was its ability to get into the air more quickly at a steeper angle, thus cutting off the longer, slower rise of more traditional planes. Although both crashes were attributed to pilot error, Bill wasn't buying it. Something was wrong with his airplane.

"There's only one thing to do," he said. "We need to ground every Learjet until we can find out what is wrong."

Not surprisingly, Bill's top executives disagreed. Who would be so foolish as to ground an entire fleet of airplanes when nobody was calling for them to do so? "Do you want to destroy the company?" they asked. "If you tell the jet owners not to fly their own planes—their expensive private planes—they will lose confidence in our product. It will ruin our reputation and destroy any hope of future sales."

"I understand that," Bill said, "but we have to find out why those planes crashed. People died."

"Well, let's conduct our own investigation," someone suggested. "We're not under any obligation to make a public announcement. Bill, please think about what you are doing."

Bill did. He went out to his jet parked in the company hangar, and he climbed into the cockpit and stared at the control panel of his amazing, intricate invention. He thought about the difficult road it had been getting his plane to this point, how as a little boy he had read Horatio Alger books and he had believed that he could accomplish something great with his life.

He recalled listening earnestly to sermons from his pastor about honesty and integrity, and about doing the right thing even when it wasn't an easy thing to do. Most of all, Bill grappled with what had gone wrong with those two downed jets.

Bill believed that the Learjet was the finest aircraft of its kind, but he knew his business associates were correct. To even hint that something was wrong with their plane could put them right out of business. Bill pondered that scenario in the dim lights of the cockpit. But then he also considered the alternative: not to admit that something could be wrong—if there was—could lead to more people dying.

He slipped out of the pilot's seat and stepped out of his plane; he had made his decision. The next day he issued a notice to all owners of Learjets around the world: don't fly your plane until our company completes an investigation.

Bill didn't stop there. He began taking his Learjet apart, piece by piece, trying to find an answer to the crashes, looking for clues, any similarity at all. He had been a Sherlock Holmes fan as a boy, so he began investigating the mystery by looking for elements that the two crashes had in common. He discovered that both crashes had taken place after the planes had taken off in warm but rainy weather. The pilots had climbed quickly to twenty-four thousand feet, leveled off, increased their speed—and then crashed.

As Bill noted the similarities, he studied the elevators, the movable parts of the Lear's tail wing that cause a plane to climb or descend. He pored over the drain holes in the part that allows rainwater to escape. He studied and studied and analyzed all his computations, and eventually he came up with a shocking discovery. Bill found that under normal conditions, the rain would drain out of the plane's elevators with no problem, but if a plane took off in warm weather and quickly climbed to twenty-four thousand feet, it was possible for the rainwater to quickly freeze before it could drain out, causing the plane's elevators to function incorrectly as it gained speed, throwing the plane out of control.

That was Bill's theory anyhow. He could have taken that theory to aeronautics experts and let them test it, but he didn't want to create any more ruckus than he already had. Clients were already canceling their orders for new Learjets. He didn't need more adverse publicity.

Bill decided to test his theory himself. He attached two-ounce weights to the elevators on his plane, simulating the effect the frozen water might have on another plane. He strapped himself into the cockpit, said a prayer, and headed down the runway. The Learjet, with Bill Lear at the controls, streaked into the sky at the usual steep angle; then at twenty-four thousand feet, Bill leveled the plane and accelerated. At first everything seemed fine as Bill's speed quickly approached 550 miles per hour, but suddenly without warning, the entire plane began to shake. Bill's instrument panel looked like a bunch of gauges gone wild. The plane began to careen out of control, and had Bill not been hanging on to the controls with all his strength, it probably would have. He quickly backed off his speed, brought the jet under control, and landed without incident.

After wiping the perspiration from his brow and giving his heart a chance to calm down, Bill knew he had the answer. A simple design change on the plane's elevator drain holes corrected the life-threatening problem. Lear sent his company mechanics all over the world at his expense, making the changes in his clients' planes. Within three days, all the Learjets were capable of flying safely again. Bill Lear passed away in 1978, but he was always quick to admit his mistakes and take steps to correct them. He wasn't afraid to say those difficult words: "I was wrong. I made a mistake. I'm sorry; please forgive me."

At some point in all of our careers, we'll have reason to say those words.

It may not be after a tragic incident like Bill Lear experienced, but it will take courage on your part and mine, nonetheless.

I once put a lot of money into a microfilm company, a minority enterprise at a time when similar businesses managed by minorities in America were rare. But it never caught on. Was I discouraged? You bet. When you've experienced a business failure, a bankruptcy, or some other type of business setback, it is tempting to think, *Why don't I just get a real job like everybody else? I can work for a company and bring home a paycheck and forget about the hassles.*

Don't let yourself fall into that trap. If you want to make a career change, that's fine. But don't let failure drive you away from your dream. Before you make any rash decisions or take any knee-jerk actions, ask yourself what lessons you can learn from that business failure. Seek to understand why the business caved in on you; if you don't, I can almost guarantee you that you will make the same mistakes again, even if you engage in a business that is totally unrelated to the business in which your original mistakes took place.

Before you walk away from your business or career, analyze honestly whether you have given it your best shot. When you don't put 100 percent of yourself into something, you are asking for failure. Especially if you put your confidence in someone who has a "can't win" attitude, or you delegate responsibility to people who are not winners or who don't really know the business or have a heart for it. Don't even listen to the guy who lists all the reasons why he can't make the sale, get the client, or do whatever it takes. If you listen to him long enough, his attitude will rub off on you!

Do something, even if you aren't sure. If you make a wrong turn, trust that the marketplace will straighten you out, and you will be able to redirect your efforts. Believe that another opportunity is coming your way and might even be right around the corner. You may have to give up on a job, on a relationship, or even on a portion of your career, but never give up on God and never give up on yourself.

WHAT DOES IT MEAN
TO BE A SUCCESS?

Success is certainly more than money, fame, or the appreciation of your peers. To me, success is helping someone else get to where I am or, better yet, to a place beyond where I am.

At the height of my first career in boxing, I loved to drive my Rolls-Royce into the inner-city of Houston and park it at the George Foreman Youth and Community Center. All the kids would come by and ask, "What kind of car is that?" I knew that many of those young people had never before seen a car like that up close, and I also knew that some of them would solve the riddle of the Rolls-Royce. They'd find out where it was made and how much it cost, and then they would begin to dream: *One day I'm going to have a car like that. Someday I can be successful too!*

After the "glory days" from my first boxing career, when I became a preacher, I still enjoyed being just one of the guys. I loved talking with every-day people and encouraging them to be their best. I knew I had something special to share with them, and it seemed they were always willing to chat with me. Ironically, a lot of people didn't recognize me from my fighting days; they simply accepted me as "George." One time I was in Nacogdoches, Texas, and I met a fellow and engaged him in a conversation about life. After a while, he asked me, "What do you do?"

"Well, I'm a preacher of the gospel."

"Really? You look like an athlete."

"I used to be a boxer," I told him.

"Hmmph, if you can box, you don't need to preach," he said matter-of-factly.

We both had a good laugh at that.

I realized that I could live without the money, fame, or a big house or fancy car. Those things were nice and I enjoyed them (and still do), but most of all, I enjoyed inspiring other people. For me, success was helping people to believe that anyone can do something great. For years I spent a lot of time with people who made relatively small amounts of money, but they had something money couldn't buy—contentment.

My wife, Joan, and I live by this truth: "Having godliness with contentment is great gain. For you brought nothing into this world, and it is certain, you will carry nothing out." If someone gave me a check for twenty billion dollars, that wouldn't make me one bit happier or more content than I was when we had next to nothing. We had peace and contentment in our hearts and minds and with our family members too.

Often when I was working on my boxing comeback, I'd fight in some town for a few thousand dollars and afterward somebody would ask me, "George, could you come to our church to speak?" or "George, before you leave, could you stop by the prison and talk to some of the men incarcerated there?" I tried to do as much of that sort of thing as I could within my time limits. I found amazing satisfaction and contentment in talking to that relatively small crowd in a church or to a few kids who had made bad choices and done foolish things that had landed them in prison. I told them my story and encouraged them to put their trust in God and live a different way than they had in the past. I shared with them some of my secrets to how they could find true contentment. No amount of acclaim in the business world or in my career could compare to the satisfaction I found in helping someone else get on the right road. To this day I gravitate toward those people—people who are satisfied, happy, and content, regardless of the conditions or circumstances in which they live.

PEOPLE NOTICE TRUE CONTENTMENT

Popular radio talk show host Michael Harris met me when I did several interviews with him during my first run as boxing's heavyweight champion of the world. I always showed up in my swanky car, wearing some outlandish suit that I thought represented success. Years later, after I had become a preacher, Michael invited me to be on his show again. This time I dressed in ordinary clothes and drove to his show in a Ford Fiesta—a basic, stripped-down compact car that I parked outside the studio.

At the time Michael was not interested in religion, but when he looked out the window and saw me pull up in the Ford Fiesta, his curiosity was piqued. Years later he told me that he wondered how a guy like me who had lived lavishly could ever be content with such ordinary, mundane things. Michael knew that when I had been riding high in my boxing career, I used to drive my fancy cars, especially my Stutz Blackhawk, and people would gather around just to look at George's car.

But after I lost everything and was rebuilding my life, a friend at church told me about a used car lot where I could find a good deal. He was right. I went to the lot, and I found the little Ford Fiesta. I asked the owner, "Have you done any work on it?"

"Not a bit," he replied.

I was surprised since I was accustomed to used car salesmen telling me how much they had done to fix up their cars so they could sell them for top dollar, whether they had really done anything to improve the cars when they came into the dealership or not. "Do you mean to tell me you haven't done anything to fix up this car?" I asked.

"Nope. Not a thing," he said straightforwardly. "Here's what happened, son. I used to get cars in here, and I'd spend a lot of money to fix them up, but then customers wouldn't believe me. Someone would look at one of those cars, and I'd tell him what I had in it, and he'd say, 'Well, I'm not pay-ing that much!'

" 'Look, I spent a lot of money to fix this car up nice,' I'd tell them, but they'd never believe me, so now I just sell a car 'as is.' "

"Do you mean to tell me that you haven't done anything at all to this car?" I asked. I was even more surprised now because the little Fiesta looked real clean.

"Nothin'," the dealer spat out with a smile. "You might want to change the oil, but other than that, it's ready to go."

I bought that little Fiesta and I sure had fun with it! I was content driving it too. When I pulled in the lot outside Michael Harris's studio, I had a look of contentment on my face, and Michael noticed. As a result, Michael became more interested in religion and eventually came to his own faith in the good Lord.

Truth is, if your contentment is found in a car, a house, any material thing, or a person, it can be wiped out in a moment. But when you have contentment that starts with God and fills your heart and mind, you can be content no matter what your circumstances.

Many of the people I met in those days were not rich financially, but they were rich in contentment. They were not complacent; they had goals, worked hard at their jobs, kept a roof over their heads, had food on the table for their families, and enjoyed wonderfully fulfilling lives.

Let me say it again: true success and significance don't depend on how much money you make. If you have contentment and you can enjoy the little things in life, you have it all. I'm convinced that some of the happiest people I have ever met are men and women who haven't made a lot of money. But they have joy. They don't complain about the stock market or politics or taxes; they just work hard, enjoy their families, and strive to make their com-munities better.

A few years ago I took an interest in the Houston Rockets basketball games, and each time I attended, a certain ticket scalper outside the arena waved and said hello to me. I'd talk to him briefly and eventually we struck up a friendship. One time as I was passing by, he called out to me, "George! George, I have something for you!" He caught up to me and handed me some coupons.

"What is this?" I asked.

"I have a little place where I sell chicken," he said. "Stop by sometime for some free chicken."

Joan and I stopped by my friend's establishment and sure enough, he had a place where he sold chicken. It was a beautiful French's Chicken franchise! After that Joan and I made a habit of stopping anytime we were in the area, sometimes going out of our way to buy some of my friend's delicious chicken. I thought I was doing him a favor and that he was just a struggling entrepreneur, but he was actually a successful businessman.

For ten years I rarely heard people talking about doom and despair. Funny, during those days few people with whom I associated made a lot of money, but they made good lives. That's what being a Knockout Entrepreneur is all about.

The secret to my success—and to yours—is finding true contentment. When you have that, you have it all!

KNOCKOUT IDEAS
TO STIMULATE YOUR SUCCESS

1. When you really stop to consider your life, what do you want it to be about?

2. *I was wrong* are some of the toughest words to say. When was the last time you said them to a friend, coworker, or family member? What was the result?

3. How much of your image of success is wrapped around money, fame, power, or material things?

4. What does contentment mean to you? How will you know when you have found it?

CHAPTER FOURTEEN

CELEBRATE YOUR SUCCESS

You have finally made it. You have achieved enough of your goals that you can kick back and enjoy some of the fruits of your labors. Now you need to know when and how to celebrate your success. As a Knockout Entrepreneur you will most likely always deal with success, so learn to mind your money and influence carefully and handle your success humbly.

Watch out for the perils of quick success. When everything is going well, keep in mind that success is not static. You have to keep working, keep growing, keep improving your product or services or developing new ones. I really don't spend a lot of time trying to manage my money. I focus my energy on trying to earn more. *Earn, earn, earn!* I tell myself. I can hire wise and trustworthy financial experts to help manage my investments. I look for people who can explain my investment portfolio in language I can understand. If a financial expert cannot tell me how my money is working for me, he or she won't be working for me for long. The financial expert's job is to help me best manage my resources. My job is to keep earning more.

If you earn one million dollars and then stop earning, you will be on your way to the poorhouse before you know it. Something is always going wrong somewhere in the financial realm. Stocks drop like heavy rocks sometimes. Even housing and real estate prices can take a hit; banks can take a loss. Internet companies have blown away faster than hitting the delete button on your computer. So don't depend on what you have; learn to think in terms of what you are going to get. The best investment you can make is your enthusiasm for earning. Think you have enough? Earn more.

"Well, isn't that being selfish, George?" someone may ask.

That all depends on what you do with what the good Lord allows you to earn.

Many people who work hard to become successful seem to forget what brought them to that point. They have all the money they need, so they purchase the best, most comfortable easy chair they can find. They sit back, prop their feet up, and get lazy. All they do is sit around in that La-Z-Boy. After a while, they get out of shape and out of touch, and they can hardly walk anymore, much less work.

Something similar happens in business, especially when you make a lot of money. If you aren't careful, you will grow complacent and no longer be able to compete. You'll grow fat with your success. In ancient times kings went out to war and conquered their enemies. Too often they came back home and celebrated their success with such drinking and carousing that all they wanted to do was lie around and be lazy. Not surprisingly, before long their enemies rose up against them and many of those kings were easily conquered.

That's one reason why I was willing to sell off my portion of the George

Foreman grill licenses. I woke up each morning and I was scared. Can you imagine that? George Foreman afraid of something? But I was. I wasn't fearful that I would run out of money. I was worried that I would not be successful at other things, that perhaps the grill was one colossal fluke, and that I could never do anything else meaningful. In some ways it was good for me to divest some of my interest in the George Foreman grill licenses. After I released the grill, I was free.

Great success can be one of the worst things that happens to someone who has worked hard to achieve his or her goals. You wake up one day, and somebody says, "They need you downtown to do an interview," and you say, "I don't want to do any more interviews. I don't *need* to do another interview."

Sometimes successful men or women say such things as, "I'm not going to take this anymore. I don't need to put up with that stuff." What has happened? They've lost perspective; they've forgotten what brought them to the party in the first place. To put it in language closer to me, it is like trying to box while sitting on your hands.

STAY HUNGRY

Knockout Entrepreneurs always have to stay hungry—not physically hungry, but hungry for the next big challenge, the next opportunity, another chance to be creative, another possibility of helping to meet a need.

How do you stay hungry when you are wonderfully successful?

My way may not be the most comfortable or the most popular, but I've always stayed hungry by being willing to sell my last option. When you have the opportunity to sell your last piece of product or your last idea, don't clutch it tenaciously. Sell it!

"But if I sell all these, I won't have anything left!" I hear you fretting.

Right! And you will have to engage your creativity once again to develop something else that will be an exciting new adventure for you. Don't wallow in your past successes. Get on to the next thing! As you do, you will enjoy a perpetual sense of excitement, and you will look forward to getting out of bed each day to see what new thing God is going to bring your way. Keep working; keep looking for new ideas; keep earning fresh income. How much money you have or don't have is irrelevant. Certainly you want to be content with whatever you have, but at the same time, if you will keep working and continue to motivate yourself, you will be much happier than you would be lying on a beach and sipping drinks with little umbrellas in them all day, or spending all your time on the golf course. Have you ever noticed that people who retire to those kinds of lifestyles often don't live too long after they've retired? Why is that? They simply got bored.

Just to have a purpose, a reason to get up in the morning and know that you have a job to go to, is stimulating. I don't really have a financial need, but I still look forward to getting out of bed each day and getting to work. I don't ever want to lose that sense of purpose I have discovered through working hard to make a living. Sometimes people ask me, "George, what has been the secret of your success? How did you do it?"

That's easy. I got up each day and worked harder than anyone else. If you want to be successful, I recommend the same prescription for you. There are no magic formulas to success. It is often just a matter of showing up. If you show up for work consistently and do a great job every day, you will be promoted. If you simply show up for class at the university, you are already far ahead of many of your peers. Study hard, do a little more work than is required, take time to meet with your professors, smile as you go along, and you will make the grade and more. But if you insist on being a sluggard, I can't help you, and I honestly don't think anyone else can either.

Get up each day, go out and work hard, and you will be a success at whatever you put your mind to do.

If you have children, you must impart this passion for success to them. Remember, if you are successful, they will take many things for granted that you never had as a child. That is to be expected, but if you don't let them know the values on which you have built your life, your success can destroy your children.

GUARD YOUR WEAK SPOTS

Maintain your humility and be aware of your weaknesses, especially weaknesses in areas of character. For instance, if you know you are tempted in the area of alcohol, don't go into the bars at hotels when you are on business trips by yourself. If you know you are vulnerable to sexual temptation, stay far away from anything or anyone who might entice you to compromise your values. Know your weaknesses and take appropriate steps to compensate for them.

Be aware of your tendency to be prideful, arrogant, or unappreciative of other people. Go out of your way to be kind to people, to say hello, or to do something helpful for them. By humbling yourself to be a servant, you can avoid developing an attitude of superiority.

Ambition can be a good thing, but it can also be destructive if it takes over your life, so you must ask yourself, *At what point does it go too far?* Study the lives of other successful people and seek to discover how they fared after they achieved a high level of success. Some handled their success well; others did not. Some kept their feet on the ground and their heads out of the clouds; others became pompous and egotistical. One of the best ways to stay down to earth is occasionally to remind yourself where you came from. The great athlete Jim Thorpe came from nothing and achieved it all. Ray Johnson was a remarkable decathlon athlete in 1958; Mary Lou Retton was a world-class gymnast. All of them had to overcome tremendous odds to achieve their success, and all carved out significant lives as a result. No doubt you will too. Remind yourself of the things you had to overcome. You no longer need to live there—thank the good Lord—but you should never forget where you came from.

Character traits make the difference, positively or negatively. Some boxers have been successful in the ring but unsuccessful in life and have unfortunately self-destructed, while others have gone on to become incredible high-profile celebrities. For instance, Jack Dempsey had an outstanding boxing career and a wonderful life after he left the sport. Joe Frazier is a good man, ambitious but not arrogant. Evander Holyfield is another man who has discovered real life outside the ring. That's what genuine success is all about.

Now that you are successful, use what you have positively. Understand, that's not always as easy as it sounds. Consider the fact that gaining a lot of money has destroyed the lives of some lottery winners. Why? They constantly wonder if people are being nice to them simply because they have a cache of money. Finding success is not enough; you have to find reality, and you have to find higher motivation.

Dave Thomas, founder of Wendy's restaurants, was a great role model for me. Dave often served as his own pitchman for his products, and his commercials worked because he was sincere. He believed in his product and anyone could tell that he enjoyed what he was doing. His enthusiasm came right through the television spots, and it was obvious he wasn't just doing this for personal wealth. What many people didn't know, though, was that Dave Thomas was orphaned at a young age and his passion in life was not simply to make a lot of money selling hamburgers; he wanted to help other kids who had experienced similar losses.

Helping other people is a big payoff for me as well. That's why I spend as much time as I can at the George Foreman Youth and Community Center, so I can help pass on the good stuff. Find some way to help other people achieve some measure of your success. You'll never be sorry you did.

I want to handle my business in such a way that the things I say and do, my business practices and the way I treat other people, will be a model for my children to emulate. That's why I take advantage of every opportunity to educate my children about how our businesses operate. A lot of parents are reluctant to draw their children into the family business. I think that is a mistake. If you knew your children were going to take over your entire business at your retirement, in what ways would you teach them your business? You better get started.

Being a good businessman and a good family man is important to me, and I enjoy the way several of our kids are involved in our businesses. But I enjoy our children who are not involved in our businesses just as much. Having the right priorities has been emphasized around the Foreman home, and the kids have picked up on that. It's fun for me to watch how those priorities are working out in their individual lives, whether it is by going to college, working for me, or getting involved in their own careers. We have made it clear to our kids that they are not merely employees in our business ventures; they are partners.

What about retirement? The question of when I will retire is not at what age, but at what income? When is the right time to retire, or not? In one sense, I'm never going to retire. I've already tried retiring several times, but I just enjoy work too much to sit around. The idea of calculating how much money my family and I are going to need to live every month and then hoping that the cost of living doesn't increase before we die and go to heaven—that's no way to live. That's fear and stagnancy, not the exciting adventure of life.

Some people want to retire so they can relax and take it easy. Some are looking forward to playing golf every day. But how long can you relax before you get bored? How much golf can you play before it grows dull and uninteresting to you? I don't know and I don't want to find out. That would be a tragedy for me, a death knell. So I keep finding new, creative, entrepreneurial ventures to explore.

KEEP LOOKING FOR FRESH OPPORTUNITIES

When I moved away from boxing, I suddenly realized how much I truly enjoyed the sport. I didn't really want to give up boxing, but it was time. My half-a-century-old body was letting me know that it was time, and if I had any doubts about it, my wife, Joan, was letting me know that it was *time*! But in the midst of walking away from boxing, I discovered the world of business. Suddenly I had a new reason to get out of bed every morning. I was on the lookout for the next new opportunity. Some of the things I did were to develop my new career; other ventures were just for the sheer enjoyment of doing them.

For example, in 2008, my son George III ("Monk") came up with the idea of doing a television reality show called *Family Foreman*—based around our daily family activities—that would air on the TV Land network. It sounded like fun and it would be new territory for us, so we decided to do it. Few things, of course, are less real than television "reality" programs. After all, it is rather strange and unnerving to wear a wireless microphone under your clothes and to have a television camera crew around your home all day long. Most indoor shots require bright television lights, so that lends an even more unnatural feel to something as simple as sitting down in the kitchen for breakfast.

Nevertheless we had memorable experiences with the show. I'm part owner of an Indy car team, the type of sleek superfast race cars that race at the Indianapolis 500, so one episode revolved around our daughter Natalie singing "God Bless America" at an Indy car race in Chicago. Her brother Monk set up the performance without Natalie's knowledge, much less approval. Natalie didn't know all the words to the song, and with less than three days' notice, she was not exactly singing her brother's praises. But Natalie is an aspiring singer, so she took it all in stride. She was nervous, but she knew she could do it.

At the race, I put my arm around her and said, "Here you go. This is your shot! Are you excited?"

"Yeah!" Natalie beamed.

"The only thing to remember is to try to make people feel good," I told her. "Okay, go get them!"

Natalie and Monk headed toward the stage. I walked to the garage area where I had a chance to encourage my race team members before the race and then went to the grandstand area where I was to do the traditional "Drivers, start your engines!" after Natalie's song.

Everything was going as planned until Natalie was introduced to the enthusiastic crowd. Just as she began singing the song in front of more than eighty thousand race fans at the track and millions more watching on television, the sound system let out a loud screeching sound caused by feedback. "God bless America . . ." *eeerrrk!* People in the stands covered their ears to avoid the shrill sound, but Natalie kept going like a pro. A lot of singers might have bolted from the stage in tears or thrown a temper tantrum, but not Natalie. When the piercing sound subsided, she picked right back up with the song and continued as though nothing had happened. Watching Natalie handle that adversity and carrying off the song so beautifully after the interruption was one of the proudest moments of my life. I mean that girl can sing!

We did a wide variety of episodes for *Family Foreman*, including one shot down at the ranch where ostensibly I wanted everyone to camp out and rough it. In truth, our ranch is almost like a second home, so there wasn't much roughing it, especially when the family got up from the campsite and left me sleeping out under the stars by myself. They all slipped inside the ranch house and snuggled into their comfortable beds.

In another episode, after I missed a date with my wife, I bought her an expensive diamond ring as a peace offering. Then I became distracted by a benefit gala we attended and I didn't do a very good job of paying attention to Joan. When I finally gave her the ring, she was unimpressed. The moral of that story is that she didn't want bling—she wanted me!

All of the shows had a subtle message about the love and importance of family. Although I'm fairly certain none of us will be nominated for Emmy Awards, the Foreman family had fun doing the series, and it brought us together for some activities we might not have done otherwise. That made the show a success for me, regardless of the ratings we garnered. It wasn't about having a wildly popular television program; it was about giving the TV audience an enjoyable experience while giving my family a chance to pursue some of their dreams as we all explored new opportunities.

Expressing creativity in new ways has always appealed to me. For instance, back in the late 1970s after I found the Lord, I also found myself spending a lot of time alone. Sometimes I woke up in the middle of the night with music running through my mind. I had visions of people singing to me, one fellow in particular singing with a guitar in the background. I'll never forget the man singing, "It was Jesus who died for me."

I didn't think much more about the music until several years later when I was driving from California to Texas by myself. I had been sorely disappointed in some of the people with whom I had been attending church in Houston, and I was having a tough time grappling with that. The people I had considered to be strong spiritual leaders were not nearly as consistent as I had believed them to be. Sure, some people in certain areas of professional boxing had disappointed me, but I regarded that as an occupational hazard. I never expected to be so hurt by people in the church.

As I drove the long trip back home, one thought plagued my mind: *I am all alone.*

I asked myself again and again, *What do I do now?* The church had been my family since leaving the boxing world. How was I going to make it?

Going along the straight flat highway, I took out a pen and began to write as I drove. The words seemed to flow out of me:

My mother used to tell me
about the God who would save men's souls;
But I could not believe her;
then she told me about his Son who had walked upon the sea;
But I could not believe her.
She was the first one who told me that story of how Jesus got up
   from the dead;
But I could not believe her.
I'll never forget the time, she told me, "Son, you know, he might not
   be there when you call him," then she whispered, "Oh, but he
   is always right on time."
But I could not believe my mother.
But now, I thank my God for showing me the truth.
He let me know that he was alive, and that his Son was, too.
Now, I can believe her, now I can believe my mother.

It was an unusual feeling, writing such things on paper. I might have thought them, but I had never actually expressed them like that. Okay, it wasn't Emily Dickinson, but it was a start—a new creative way for me to say some things that matter to me.

During the years I continued writing, expressing some of my deep, inner spiritual thoughts and feelings. From time to time, I had my kids at church take some of my words and put them to melodies, and they would sing them for Sunday services and at street meetings in the inner-city of Houston.

Around the late 1990s, I decided to put some of my lyrics on an album. No, I didn't want to sing (although I enjoy singing), but my idea was to have other people from all walks of life, from a wide variety of musical genres, join me on the album.

My good friend Tony Fritsch was a placekicker for the Dallas Cowboys. Tony had grown up in Austria, playing soccer almost from the time he could run and kick a ball. When Tony first joined the Cowboys, Coach Tom Landry asked him to kick a few field goals for him in practice. "Which foot do you want me to kick them with?" Tony asked. Coach Landry knew he had found his kicker!

When I told Tony about my idea for recording my lyrics, he said, "George, why don't we get the Vienna Boys' Choir?"

Although I had been to Austria and had met the choir, I never would have dreamed of asking them to appear on my album, but Tony was insistent. He was still a big hero in Austria, and he promised to help me make it happen. "They'll love it, George. And you know they will do a fantastic job!" he exclaimed.

So I invited the Vienna Boys' Choir to appear on my album, and they accepted. We went into the studio and recorded a double-disc set of inspiring gospel songs. The album was titled *Inspirations*, and we put it out on Trauma Records.

Although I didn't sing on the project, I played the role of host and presenter, providing narration on an eleven-song compilation of classical, operatic music featuring the Vienna Boys' Choir and the well-known operatic tenor Ramon Vargas, as well as mezzo-soprano Domino Blue. Interspersed between songs such as "It Was Jesus Who Died for Me" and "Without Jesus," both featuring Ramon, I shared a bit of my life experiences and how God had transformed my life, and I offered encouragement based on my experiences for others to find a similar relationship with Jesus. Behind the Boys' Choir, Ramon, Domino, and me were the lush sounds of the Vienna Festival Symphony Orchestra.

Occasionally while we were working on the album, I would look around and almost pinch myself to make sure it was real. I thought of all the great vocalists and artists who had dreamed of the Vienna Boys' Choir singing their songs, and here the choir chose to work with me. I was nearly overwhelmed. And I was certainly honored by those great voices and musicians using their talents to help me tell my story—which really isn't mine at all, but is His story.

Also on the second disc, I had the sounds of the late 1960s hit "Oh Happy Day," by the Edwin Hawkins Singers and an eclectic set of previously released material including Aretha Franklin singing "You'll Never Walk Alone," Yolanda Adams singing "Thank You," B. J. Thomas doing "Let There Be Peace on Earth," and Lee Greenwood performing "How Great Thou Art." It was quite a collection, and it was a marvelous way of expressing the hope we had all discovered in God.

BECOME A GIVER

I tell that story to encourage you to do more than make a good living. Now that you've made money, what are you going to do with it? Let me offer a suggestion: become a giver. The George Foreman Youth and Community Center has helped me more than I have helped the young people who go there. Helping young boys find meaning and purpose, giving them a safe place to compete in a good atmosphere, and watching them grow up to be fine young men are some of the most rewarding things I've ever done. I also enjoy giving to institutions of higher learning. I believe in education, and I've noticed that most people who do well in life usually have a good education.

I've enjoyed helping other hardworking entrepreneurs get a break. I meet a number of people who have innovative ideas for products or services, ideas that the world needs, but the fledgling businessman doesn't have the money to capitalize his dream. Occasionally I'll secretly invest in such a venture to help out a talented, dedicated person. I like to do such things without fanfare, and my favorite way to help someone like that is in a way that he or she never knows that I have been the benefactor. Sometimes I'll enter into a business relationship with a new venture and the excitement is like working toward the heavyweight championship all over again!

Giving motivates you. It makes you feel that you are doing something worthwhile, that you are needed. I've also discovered that every time I give to others—whether I give my time, money, or influence—God has ways of bringing back more to me. And usually He gives back more than I gave in the first place. I can't lose on that deal! I tell people, "If you really want to become successful, become a giver. Help someone else. Extend your hand of charity."

Work to be a success, always look for ways to give, and you will be amazed at how it comes back to you. The Bible tells us, "Give, and it shall be given unto you; good measure, pressed down, and shaken together, and running over, shall men give into your bosom. For with the same measure that ye mete withal it shall be measured to you again."[1] Notice that "men"— other people—will give to you. People will want to help you, they'll want to do business with you, and they'll want you on their team in their company because you are a giver. Whether you get anything in return or not, it is still a blessing to give.

It really is more blessed to give than to receive. We all like to receive blessings, but you will find more joy, happiness, contentment, and significance in giving than you have ever found in receiving. Don't wait for a holiday, birthday, or a special reason; make giving a way of life.

Sure, there will always be people who try to take advantage of your generosity. Some people will say, "You're so successful, and you have so much, can't you help me?" They don't want you to teach them or to give them a good idea, an opportunity, or a word of encouragement; they basically want a handout. Some people will try to make you feel guilty for being successful.

Certainly you want to be sensitive to people who are genuinely in need. The Good Book teaches that if you see someone who is destitute, who doesn't have enough to provide for his or her daily needs, and is out in the cold, and you say, "Go and be blessed," it is an insult to that person and to God. Similarly the Bible says that our faith without works is dead. People shouldn't have to beg for us to help them when we have been so blessed and have so much.

At the same time, you aren't really helping others by giving them money to perpetuate their negative habits or to pay for their foolishness. You help others only when you help them take responsibility for their lives. When people ask for your contributions, do your best to evaluate whether the need is real. Understand that you have gotten ahead in the game and to whom much is given, much is required. Somebody probably sacrificed to help you, and now you may have a similar opportunity to reach out a hand to help your brother or sister.

If people are doing all they can, working hard, and sincerely trying to manage their lives by good principles, do all you can to help. But if helping merely perpetuates laziness or unwise habits, you are wasting your time and money and only extending the problem by continuing to dole out money, time, or resources to somebody who is not doing his part. The only thing worse than someone having a lot and not helping other people is somebody who expects you to help her, just because you have something, yet is unwilling to do anything to improve the situation.

There are lots of ways to help people that don't cost a dime. Sometimes taking an interest in someone or saying an encouraging word can be worth far more than money. Some of my relatives have several young boys. One boy was picking on a smaller boy, who was always crying.

The next time the bigger boys started picking on the little boy, he came running to me. I said, "Don't you worry about hitting anyone. I'll be the one who is looking out for you. I'll be protecting you."

That little boy stood up straight and you'd have thought I had given him a million dollars.

Now when some of the other boys start picking on some of the small boys, that little eight-year-old goes over to the younger kids and says, "Don't you worry; I'll be protecting you." What is he doing? He's giving what was given to him.

Maybe you have something you can give. Maybe you can be a big brother or a big sister to a child who needs a positive role model or a bit of encouragement. Perhaps you can volunteer to help at a homeless shelter. Regardless of the method, find a way to give to others.

It's not merely a matter of giving something back. Frankly, if you earned your money legally, you are under no obligation to give anything back. On the other hand, if you didn't earn it legally, you are going to lose it all eventually. But if your wealth has come from working hard, taking risks, and being creative, don't feel guilty about what you have.

God loves a cheerful giver, and you can never outgive God. The more you give, the more He will pour into your lap. So don't give out of guilt; don't give because someone manipulates you into giving. Give because it pleases God. Give because you want to. Give because giving feels good deep inside. Don't just give till it hurts; give till it feels good! Invest generously in things that matter. It is an absolutely amazing truth: the more you give, the more you receive. And the cycle continues.

More and more these days, I think about leaving a legacy. So often we read of movie stars or gifted singers or fine athletes simply disappearing when their star burns out. It is almost as though they never really lived because they left so little behind for the next generation. I want to do something that leaves a legacy not just for boxers but for everyone. One day, after I've been in heaven for quite a while, I want to look down and notice someone looking up "George Foreman" in the library or on the Internet. "Wow," I can hear him saying, "look what this boxer did! And he was a preacher too!" In the meantime I'm going to get up every morning and look for a new challenge.

Not long ago I called my friend Muhammad Ali. I said, "Muhammad, I think I can really get you now in a rematch."

He sort of laughed and said, "George, you're crazy!" Ali is in his midsixties and doesn't speak real clearly these days due to Parkinson's disease, but he spoke kindly and said, "George, I'm coming to see you."

I said, "Come on!" So don't be surprised if you see Muhammad and me lacing up the gloves one more time.

Why?

Because Knockout Entrepreneurs never quit.

Along with the other principles I've shared with you in these pages, that is one of the key secrets to my success. As I said in the beginning, these truths are not on trial. I know they work. They have worked for me, they work for my family members, and they will work for you. Begin today to implement even a few of these ideas in your life and you will discover whole new dimensions of success, happiness, and significance. And you too will enjoy the life and legacy of the Knockout Entrepreneur.

KNOCKOUT IDEAS
TO STIMULATE YOUR SUCCESS

1. How are you guarding against complacency in your life? What specific activities or pursuits do you need to begin in order to avoid success going to your head (or your waistline)?

2. Giving always does more for you than receiving does. Look around and find several people to whom you might give. Remember, there are a variety of ways you can give, even if you cannot contribute financially. You can give your time to a worthy cause; you can give love to a senior citizen who has nobody to care for him or her. My wife and I enjoy giving anonymously to a needy person. We know that God, our heavenly Father, who sees what we have done in secret, will reward us openly.

3. Creative people look forward to each new day because they are always looking for the next opportunity. What new opportunities have you pursued lately? Get up each day next week looking for a new way to do something of lasting significance.

Chapter 1

1. This story can be found in its entirety in the Bible (1 Samuel 30:1–19).

Chapter 2

1. See my book *God in My Corner* (Nashville: Thomas Nelson, 2007) for the full story.
2. Janice Reals Ellig and William J. Morin, *Driving the Career Highway* (Nashville: Thomas Nelson, 2007), 12.
3. See George Foreman, *God in My Corner.*

Chapter 3

1. Jack Canfield, *The Success Principles* (New York: Harper Collins, 2005), 340.

Chapter 6

1. Adapted from Dave Ramsey, Financial Peace University, audio series (Brentwood, TN: Lampo Group, 2004).
2. This statement is from Norman Vincent Peale, quoted by Pat Williams, *How to Be Like Rich DeVos* (Deerfield Beach, FL: Health Communications, Inc., 2004), 253.
3. Alvin Toffler, *Future Shock* (New York: Random House, 1970).

Chapter 7

1. Brian Tracy, *The Psychology of Selling* (Nashville: Thomas Nelson, 2004), 70.

Chapter 8

1. Matthew 5:5.
2. Scott McKain, *What Customers Really Want* (Nashville: Thomas Nelson, 2005), ix.
3. Proverbs 19:11 NASB.

Notes

Chapter 9
1. Donald Soderquist, *The Wal-Mart Way* (Nashville: Thomas Nelson, 2005), 5.
2. Zig Ziglar, *See You at the Top* (Gretna, LA: Pelican Publishing Company, 1974), 382.

Chapter 10
1. Pat Williams, *How to Be Like Rich DeVos* (Deerfield Beach, FL: Health Communications, Inc., 2004), 45.

Chapter 12
1. Charles E. Jones, *The Books You Read* (Harrisburg, PA: Executive Books, 1985), 1.

Chapter 14
1. Luke 6:38 KJV.

ACKNOWLEDGMENTS

Getting good people on your team is an important part of becoming a Knockout Entrepreneur, and I've been blessed to have some exceptionally great teammates on this project. My son George Foreman III ("Monk") deserves special thanks for his unselfish commitment of time, ideas, and energy to this book.

My friend, attorney, and media agent Henry Holmes was so helpful in working with literary agent Mark Sweeney, of Mark Sweeney and Associates, to put a great deal together with the fine folks at Thomas Nelson Publishers. Thanks to all.

Special thanks to our editorial team at Thomas Nelson—Joel Miller, Kristen Parrish, and Heather Skelton—for not giving up on this book, and for helping Ken Abraham and me to make *Knockout Entrepreneur* a practical, helpful, inspirational read.

Acknowledgments

Special thanks, too, to Leon Dreimann for passing on the important reminder: "There is no good deal unless everyone is happy."

And of course, I extend my heartiest thanks to my wife, Joan, and the ten Foreman children. You make my dreams come true every day. Most of all, I thank the Good Lord for loving me, and for teaching me everything I know about being a Knockout Entrepreneur.

 GEORGE FOREMAN, one of the world's most beloved athletes and personalities is an ordained minister and the author of 10 books. He has made millions from infomercials marketing the infamous George Foreman Lean Mean Grilling Machine, which has sold more than 100 million units to date. He has also launched a number of successful products, services and franchises, and the list continues to grow.

 KEN ABRAHAM is the collaborator on ten *New York Times* best sellers, including *God in My Corner* with George Foreman; *Let's Roll!* with Lisa Beamer, widow of United Flight 93 hero Todd Beamer; *Magnificent Desolation* with Apollo 11 astronaut Buzz Aldrin; *A Heart to Serve* with U.S. Senator Bill Frist; *Against All Odds* with Chuck Norris; and *Billy*, the previously untold story of young Billy Graham.